The Original
Summer Bridge Activities™

Second to Third Grade

SBA was created by
Michele D. Van Leeuwen

written by
Julia Ann Hobbs
Carla Dawn Fisher

illustrations by
Magen Mitchell
Amanda Sorensen

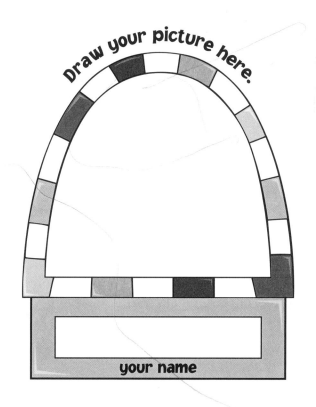

Draw your picture here.

your name

D1622140

Summer Learning Staff
Clareen Arnold, Lori Davis, Melody Feist, Aimee Hansen, Christopher Kugler,
Kristina Kugler, Molly McMahon, Paul Rawlins, Liza Richards, Linda Swain

Design
Andy Carlson, Robyn Funk

Cover Art
Karen Maizel, Amanda Sorensen

ISBN: 978-1-59441-728-3

Super Summer Science pages © 2002 The Wild Goose Company and Carson-Dellosa.

20 19 18 17 16 15 14 13 12 11

Dear Parents,

The summer months are a perfect time to reconnect with your child on many levels after a long school year. Your personal involvement is so important to your child's immediate and long-term academic success. No matter how wonderful your child's classroom experience is, your involvement outside the classroom will make it that much better!

Summer Bridge Activities™ is the original summer workbook developed to help parents support their children academically while away from school, and we strive to improve the content, the activities, and the resources to give you the highest quality summer learning materials available. Ten years ago, we introduced **Summer Bridge Activities**™ to a small group of teachers and parents after I had successfully used it to help my first grader prepare for the new school year. It was a hit then, and it continues to be a hit now! Many other summer workbooks have been introduced since, but **Summer Bridge Activities**™ continues to be the one that both teachers and parents ask for most. We take our responsibility as the leader in summer education seriously and are always looking for new ways to make summer learning more fun, more motivating, and more effective to help make your child's transition to the new school year enjoyable and successful!

We are now excited to offer you even more bonus summer learning materials online at www.**SummerBridgeActivities**.com! This site has great resources for both parents and kids to use on their own and together. An expanded summer reading program where kids can post their own book reviews, writing and reading contests with great prizes, assessment tests, travel packs, and even games are just a few of the additional resources that you and your child will have access to with the included **Summer Bridge Activities**™ Online Pass Code.

Summer Learning has come a long way over the last 10 years, and we are glad that you have chosen to use **Summer Bridge Activities**™ to help your children continue to discover the world around them by using the classroom skills they worked so hard to obtain!

Have a wonderful summer!

Michele Van Leeuwen and the Summer Learning Staff!

Hey Kids!

We bet you had a great school year!
Congratulations on all your hard work! We just want to say
that we're proud of the great things you did this year, and we're excited
to have you spend time with us over the summer. Have fun with your
Summer Bridge Activities™ workbook, and visit us online at
www.**SummerBridgeActivities**.com for more fun, cool, and exciting stuff!

Have a great summer!

The T. O. C. (Table of Contents)

Official Pass Code

rh1110f

Log on to www.SummerBridgeActivities.com and join!

Sections of SBA

☀ There are three sections in SBA: the first and second review, the third previews.

☀ Each section begins with an SBA Motivational Calendar.

☀ Each day your child will complete an activity in reading, writing, math, and language. The activities become progressively more challenging.

☀ Each page is numbered by day.

Here's what you will find inside

Summer Bridge Activities™

Exercises in **Summer Bridge Activities**™ (SBA) are easy to understand and presented in fun and creative ways that motivate children to review familiar skills while being progressively challenged. In addition to basic skills in reading, writing, math, and language arts, SBA contains activities that challenge and reinforce skills in geography and science!

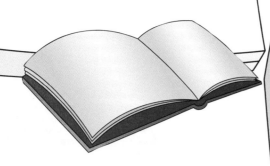

Daily exercises review and preview skills in reading, writing, math, and language arts, with additional activities in geography and science. Activities are presented in half-page increments so kids do not get overwhelmed and are divided into three sections to correlate with traditional summer vacation.

Bonus Super Summer Science pages provide hands-on science activities.

A Summer Reading List introduces kids to some of today's popular titles as well as the classics. Kids can rate books they read and log on to www.**SummerBridgeActivities**.com to post reviews, find more great titles, and participate in national reading and writing contests!

Motivational Calendars begin each section and help kids achieve all summer long.

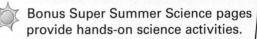

Discover Something New lists offer fun and creative activities that teach kids with their hands and get them active and learning.

Grade-specific flashcards provide a great way to reinforce basic skills in addition to the written exercises.

Removable Answer Pages ensure that parents know as much as their kids!

A Certificate of Completion for parents to sign congratulates kids for their work and welcomes them to the grade ahead.

A grade-appropriate, official Summer Fun pass code gives kids and parents online access to more bonus games, contests, and resources at www.**SummerBridgeActivities**.com.

Here are some groups who say our books are great!

Mr. Fredrickson

10 Ways to Maximize
The Original Summer Bridge Activities™

First, let your child explore the book. Flip through the pages and look at the activities with your child to help him become familiar with the book.

Help select a good time for reading or working on the activities. Suggest a time before your child has played outside and becomes too tired to do the work.

Provide any necessary materials. A pencil, ruler, eraser, crayons, or reference works may be required.

Offer positive guidance. Remember, the activities are not meant to be tests. You want to create a relaxed and positive attitude toward learning. Work through at least one example on each page with your child. "Think aloud" and show your child how to solve problems.

Give your child plenty of time to think. You may be surprised by how much children can do on their own.

Stretch your child's thinking beyond the page. If you are reading a book, you might ask, "What do you think will happen next?" or "What would you do if this happened to you?" Encourage your child to talk about her interests and observations about the world around her.

Reread stories and occasionally flip through completed pages. Completed pages and books will be a source of pride to your child and will help show how much he accomplished over the summer.

Read and work on activities while outside. Take the workbook out in the backyard or on a family campout. It can be fun wherever you are!

Encourage siblings, relatives, and neighborhood friends to help with reading and activities. Other children are often perfect for providing the one-on-one attention necessary to reinforce reading skills.

Give plenty of approval! Stickers and stamps are effective for recognizing a job well done. At the end of the summer, your child can feel proud of her accomplishments and will be eager for school to start.

Skills List

Language Arts/Reading

- [ ] Recognizes the difference between consonants and vowels
- [ ] Recognizes y as a vowel
- [ ] Recognizes blends: bl, br, cl, cr, dr, fl, fr, gl, gr, pl, pr, scr, sk, sl, sm, sn, sp, spl, spr, st, str, sw, tr, tw
- [ ] Recognizes hard and soft c and g
- [ ] Sounds out words
- [ ] Recognizes compound words
- [ ] Discriminates rhyming words
- [ ] Recognizes antonyms, synonyms, and homonyms
- [ ] Recognizes nouns
- [ ] Recognizes verbs
- [ ] Recognizes adjectives
- [ ] Recognizes pronouns
- [ ] Recognizes articles
- [ ] Recognizes helping verbs
- [ ] Recognizes subject and predicate
- [ ] Knows how to create contractions
- [ ] Knows correct abbreviations
- [ ] Knows how to form plurals with s and es
- [ ] Can divide words into syllables
- [ ] Can identify the main idea of a story
- [ ] Can identify the setting of a story
- [ ] Can identify the conclusion of a story
- [ ] Draws illustrations to match sentences
- [ ] Uses correct punctuation: period, question mark, exclamation point
- [ ] Identifies prefixes and suffixes
- [ ] Groups words into categories
- [ ] Is beginning to read and write for pleasure

Parent:

Exercises for these skills can be found inside **Summer Bridge Activities**™ and can be used for extra practice. The skills lists are a great way to discover your child's strengths or what skills may need additional reinforcement.

Skills List

Math

- [ ] Recognizes numbers to 1,000
- [ ] Completes simple patterns
- [ ] Reads number words to 100
- [ ] Can sequence events
- [ ] Can write number sentences using +, −, and =
- [ ] Knows addition facts to 18
- [ ] Knows subtraction facts to 18
- [ ] Can read and create a graph
- [ ] Understands place value in the ones place
- [ ] Understands place value in the tens place
- [ ] Understands place value in the hundreds place
- [ ] Performs two-digit addition, no regrouping
- [ ] Performs two-digit subtraction, no regrouping
- [ ] Performs three-digit addition, no regrouping
- [ ] Performs three-digit subtraction, no regrouping
- [ ] Performs two-digit addition, with regrouping
- [ ] Performs two-digit subtraction, with regrouping
- [ ] Performs three-digit addition, with regrouping
- [ ] Performs three-digit subtraction, with regrouping
- [ ] Performs addition with three single-digit addends, no regrouping
- [ ] Performs addition with three single-digit addends, with regrouping
- [ ] Knows relation and comparison symbols: <, >, =
- [ ] Recognizes money: penny, nickel, dime, quarter, half-dollar, dollar
- [ ] Knows the value of money: penny, nickel, dime, quarter, half-dollar, dollar
- [ ] Can count money using coins in combination
- [ ] Can perform money addition problems using a decimal point
- [ ] Can tell time in five-minute intervals
- [ ] Can measure using inches
- [ ] Can measure using centimeters
- [ ] Can identify and write fractions
- [ ] Uses problem-solving strategies to complete math problems

Summertime = Reading Time!

We all know how important reading is, but this summer show kids how GREAT the adventures of reading really are! Summer learning and summer reading go hand-in-hand, so here are a few ideas to get you up and going:

Encourage your child to read out loud to you and make a theatrical performance out of even the smallest and simplest read. Have fun with reading and impress the family at the campsite next to you at the same time!

Establish a time to read together each day. Make sure and ask each other about what you are reading and try to relate it to something that may be going on within the family.

Show off! Let your child see you reading for enjoyment and talk about the great things that you are discovering from what you read. Laugh out loud, stamp your feet—it's summertime!

Sit down with your child and establish a summer reading program. Use our cool Summer Reading List and Summer Reading Program at www.**SummerBridgeActivities**.com, or visit your local bookstore and, of course, your local library. Encourage your child to select books on topics he is interested in and on his reading level. A rule of thumb for selecting books at the appropriate reading level is to choose a page and have your child read it out loud. If he doesn't know five or more of the words on the page, the book may be too difficult.

Books to Read

 The Summer Reading List has a variety of titles, including some found in the Accelerated Reader Program.

We recommend parents read to pre-kindergarten through 1st grade children 5–10 minutes each day and then ask questions about the story to reinforce comprehension. For higher grade levels, we suggest the following daily reading times: grades 1–2, 10–20 min.; grades 2–3, 20–30 min.; grades 3–4, 30–45 min.; grades 4–6, 45–60 min.

 It is important to decide an amount of reading time and write it on the SBA Motivational Calendar.

Use your surroundings (wherever you are) to show your child how important reading is on a daily basis. Read newspaper articles, magazines, stories, and road maps during the family vacation...just don't get lost!

Find books that tie into your child's experiences. If you are going fishing or boating, find a book on the subject to share. This will help your child learn and develop interests in new things.

Get library cards! Set a regular time to visit the library and encourage your child to have her books read and ready to return so she is ready for the next adventure! Let your child choose her own books. It will encourage her to read and pursue her own interests.

Make up your own stories! This is great fun and can be done almost anywhere—in the car, on camping trips, in a canoe, on a plane! Encourage your child to tell the story with a beginning, middle, AND end! To really challenge each other, start with the end, then middle, and then the beginning—yikes!

Summer Bridge Activities™

Summer Reading List

Fill in the stars and rate your favorite (and not so favorite) books here and online at
www.SummerBridgeActivities.com!

1 = I struggled to finish this book.
2 = I thought this book was pretty good.
3 = I thought this book rocked!
4 = I want to read this book again and again!

Nice New Neighbors
Brandenberg, Franz

Aunt Eater's Mystery Vacation
Cushman, Doug

Ruby's Wish
Bridges, Shirin Yim

More Spaghetti, I Say!
Gelman, Rita

Ruby lives in China with her grandfather and his large family. The family tutor will teach any of the 100 grandchildren, but Ruby wants to go to university. Will she get her wish?

Today Was a Terrible Day
Giff, Patricia Reilly

Angelina Ballerina
Holabird, Katherine

Penrod's Picture
Christian, Mary Blount

Don't Forget the Bacon!
Hutchins, Pat

Chang's Paper Pony
Coerr, Eleanor

The Foolish Giant
Coville, Bruce and Katherine

John Henry, an American Legend
Keats, Ezra Jack

Stan the Hot Dog Man
Kessler, Ethel and Leonard

Here Comes the Strikeout

Kessler, Leonard P.

The Smallest Cow in the World

Paterson, Katherine

The Chanukkah Guest

Kimmel, Eric A.

Harry's Visit

Porte, Barbara Ann

Humphrey, Albert, and the Flying Machine

Lasky, Kathryn

Humphrey and Albert think going to the princess's birthday party will be boring. But they couldn't be more wrong.

Runaway Pony

Ruepp, Krista

When Anna's pony bolts at the sound of a tractor, she turns to Grandmother to help track him down.

The Stonecutter: A Japanese Folk Tale

McDermott, Gerald

A Big Fat Enormous Lie

Sharmat, Marjorie Weinman

Zack's Alligator

Mozelle, Shirley

Imogene's Antlers

Small, David

The Teeny Tiny Woman

O'Connor, Jane

The Zabajaba Jungle

Steig, William

Join the SBA Kids Summer Reading Club!

Quick! Get Mom or Dad to help you log on and join the SBA Kids Summer Reading Club. You can find more great books, tell your friends about your favorite titles, and even win cool prizes! Log on to www.SummerBridgeActivities.com **and sign up today.**

Book cover from HUMPHREY, ALBERT, AND THE FLYING MACHINE, text copyright © 2004 by Kathryn Lasky Knight, illustrations copyright © 2004 by John Manders, reproduced by permission of Harcourt, Inc.
Book cover from RUNAWAY PONY by Krista Ruepp, Illustrated by Ulrike Heyne. (c) 2005. Published by Chronicle Books, LLC.

Summer Bridge Activities™

Motivational Calendar

Month

My parents and I decided that if I complete
15 days of **Summer Bridge Activities**™ and
read _____ minutes a day, my incentive/reward will be:

Child's Signature _____ Parent's Signature_____

Day 1	☆	📖	____	Day 9	☆	📖	____
Day 2	☆	📖	____	Day 10	☆	📖	____
Day 3	☆	📖	____	Day 11	☆	📖	____
Day 4	☆	📖	____	Day 12	☆	📖	____
Day 5	☆	📖	____	Day 13	☆	📖	____
Day 6	☆	📖	____	Day 14	☆	📖	____
Day 7	☆	📖	____	Day 15	☆	📖	____
Day 8	☆	📖	____				

Child: Color the ☆ for daily activities completed.
Color the 📖 for daily reading completed.

Parent: Initial the ____ when all activities are complete.

1   © Summer Bridge Activities™ 2–3

Discover Something New!

 1 Sign up for summer classes at community education departments or local parks.

 2 Make a chart for summer chores with incentives.

 3 Write to a relative about your summer plans.

 4 Check the library for free children's programs.

 5 Boost reading—make labels for household objects.

 6 Bubble fun: one-third cup liquid dishwashing soap, plus two quarts water. Use cans or pipe cleaners for dippers.

Fun Activity Ideas to Go Along with the First Section!

 7 Make up a story at dinner. Each person adds a new paragraph.

 8 Learn about the summer solstice. Time the sunrise and sunset.

 9 Shop together—use a calculator to compare prices per pound.

 10 Start a journal of summer fun.

 11 Zoo contest—find the most African animals.

 12 Tune up those bikes. Wash 'em, too.

 13 Arrange photo albums.

 14 Play flashlight tag.

 15 Check out a science book—try some experiments.

Write to 200.

101	102	103	104	105	106	107	108	109	110
111	112	113	114	115	116	117	118	119	120
121	122	123	124	125	126	127	128	129	130
131	132	133	134	135	136	137	138	139	140
141	142	143	144	145	146	147	148	149	150
	153								160
				165					170
									180
					186				190
191							198		200

Contractions. Write the words found in each contraction.

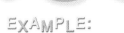

EXAMPLE:

1. we're __we are__
2. aren't __are not__
3. I've __I have__
4. you're __you are__
5. it's __it is__
6. I'll __I will__
7. we'll __we will__
8. she's __she is__
9. you've __you have__
10. won't __will not__
11. I'd __I would__
12. I'm __I am__
13. isn't __is not__
14. let's __let us__

✓

14/14

Fill in the blanks with a synonym from the Word Bank that has almost the same meaning as the underlined word in the sentence.

EXAMPLE: **1.** Here comes the <u>furry</u> cat. _____**fuzzy**_____

Word Bank

like
fuzzy
silly
largest
watch
turn
yell
leaped
unhappy
scared

2. He <u>jumped</u> out of the car. _____

3. Let's clap and <u>shout</u> for our team. _____

4. I <u>enjoy</u> watching ball games. _____

5. Were the children <u>frightened</u>? _____

6. The <u>sad</u> man was crying. _____

7. Did you <u>see</u> the frog jump? _____

8. He is riding the <u>biggest</u> horse. _____

9. Watch the top <u>spin</u> around. _____

10. Did you see that <u>funny</u> movie? _____

Write <u>person</u>, <u>place</u>, or <u>thing</u> after each sentence to identify the underlined noun.

1. The children left <u>school</u> early today. _____

2. They went to the <u>park</u> to play soccer. _____

3. The <u>teacher</u> watched the children play. _____

PERSON

4. A <u>squirrel</u> climbed the tree. _____

PLACE

5. The boys and girls rowed a <u>boat</u>. _____

6. One <u>girl</u> went down the slide. _____

THING

7. The <u>boy</u> was feeding the ducks. _____

Add or subtract.

7	0	8	6	9	9	7
+ 2	+ 3	+ 3	+ 2	+ 0	+ 1	+ 3
9	3	11	8	9	10	10

3	5	5	10	7	6	9
− 2	− 0	− 2	− 2	− 3	− 4	− 5
1	5	3	8	4	2	4

5	6	7	8	2	5	10
− 3	+ 4	− 2	− 4	+ 2	+ 5	− 5
2	2	5	4	4	10	5

Fill in the missing blends.

| fl, pl, bl, spr, sl, sk, sn, st, dr, br, pr, fr, pl, gr, cr |

1. The red and blue ____owers we ____anted will ____oom in the ____ing.

2. The boys and girls like to go ____edding and ice ____ating when it ____ows.

3. That ____ory is about a ____agon who ____eathed fire and a princess who kissed a ____og, then turned him into a ____ince.

4. My yellow, pur____e, and ____een ____ayons ____oke when I ____opped them on the ____oor.

Read the story. Number the events in the order they happened.

The Alarm Clock

Rob was sleeping when his alarm clock started ringing. He jumped up, made his bed, and washed his face. Rob put on his clothes and started down the stairs to go eat breakfast. When he passed the window in the hall, he saw that it was still night. "Oh, no," he said, "my alarm clock went off at the wrong time!" Rob went back to his bedroom and got back in bed.

5	Rob went back to bed.
1	Rob's alarm clock rang.
4	Rob saw that it was still night.
2	Rob made his bed and washed his face.
3	Rob started down to breakfast.

Read the words below. Choose a word from the box that describes each group of words below. Write the word in the blank.

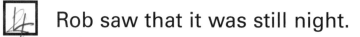
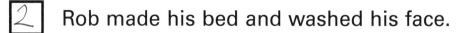

| ~~weather~~ | ~~flavors~~ | ~~animals~~ |
| ~~drinks~~ | ~~months~~ | ~~numbers~~ |

| cow, horse, goat | chocolate, berry, vanilla | one, nine, twenty |
| animals | flavors | numbers |

| rain, snow, sun | February, July, October | milk, juice, soda pop |
| weather | months | drinks |

Write the correct time on the small clocks and draw hands on the big clocks.

12:00

11 : 00

9:30

B⁻

2 : 30

6:00

7 : 30

Match the definition to the word with the same meaning.

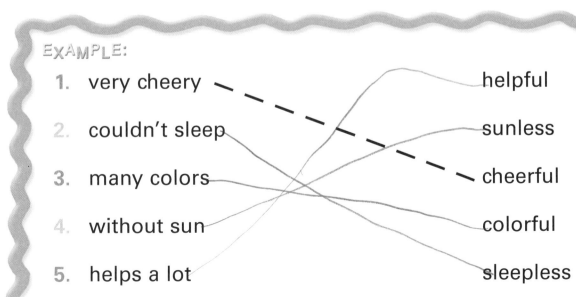

EXAMPLE:

1. very cheery   helpful

2. couldn't sleep   sunless

3. many colors   cheerful

4. without sun   colorful

5. helps a lot   sleepless

The words in these sentences are mixed up. Write them correctly. Don't forget to add capital letters and the correct ending punctuation mark: (.) or (?).

1. <u>birds do live where</u>

   _____

2. <u>very my hard works dad</u>

   _____

3. <u>swim can like fish a i</u>

   _____

4. <u>green grass the is</u>

   _____

5. <u>water do fish in live</u>

   _____

Color in the circle to show the correct spelling.

EXAMPLE:

1. ● a. what   ○ b. wat   ○ c. whut

2. ○ a. whare   ○ b. where   ○ c. whar

3. ○ a. when   ○ b. wen   ○ c. whene

4. ○ a. wiye   ○ b. wye   ○ c. why

Write the problem; then answer the question: How many in all?

 EXAMPLE:

_6_ + _3_ = _9_   _9_ worms in all

___ + ___ = ___   ____ birds in all

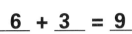

___ + ___ = ___   ____ crayons in all

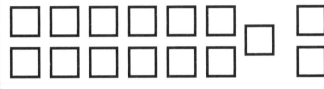

___ + ___ = ___   ____ fish in all

___ + ___ = ___   ____ balloons in all

___ + ___ = ___   ____ boxes in all

Finish these words by drawing a line to the correct ending. Write the words.

EXAMPLE:

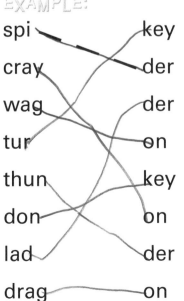

spi   key
cray   der
wag   der
tur   on
thun   key
don   on
lad   der
drag   on

spider
crayon
wagon
turkey
thunder
donkey
ladder
dragon

Fill in the blank with the correct word to complete the sentence.

1. Cats are _____ animals.
    freely   friendly   friend

2. I'd _____ help you feed your cat.
    gladly   highly   gladder

3. Matt called _____ for his cat.
    loud   loudly   tightly

4. Cats like to _____.
    playing   play   clay

5. My friend's cat _____ all day.
    sleeps   sleeping   beeps

Singular (one) or Plural (more than one). Use both forms of the word and label them correctly.

EXAMPLE:

a.	birds	— **more**	bird	— **one**
b.	girl	— **one**	girls	— **more**

1.	trees	— **more**		—
2.	boxes	— _____	_____	— _____
3.	wheel	— **one**	wheels	— _____
4.	ape	— _____	_____	— _____
5.	shoes	— _____	shoe	— **one**
6.	peach	— _____	_____	— _____
7.	nickels	— **more**	nickel	— _____
8.	plum	— _____	_____	— _____

Circle the coins that equal the correct amount.

34¢ =

72¢ =

25¢ =

49¢ =

18¢ =

Write the missing numerals in each row.

1. 51, ___, 53, 54, 55, ___, 57, ___

2. 58, 59, ___, 61, ___, 63, 64, 65, ___

3. 66, 67, ___, 69, ___, 71, 72, 73, ___

4. 74, ___, 76, 77, ___, 79, ___ 81, ___

Here is a silly story. Put a (.), (?), or (!) at the end of each sentence. Make the first letter of each sentence a capital. Then, draw a picture of this "silly thing" the way you imagine it looks.

I saw a very silly thing. It had a very funny shape. It did not make any noise. It had spots that changed color and big feet with green toes. It had little hands and a big, fat, pink nose. I hope it doesn't hurt me. Maybe it will be nice. We might become friends and play. I wonder what it likes to eat. I hope it's not me!

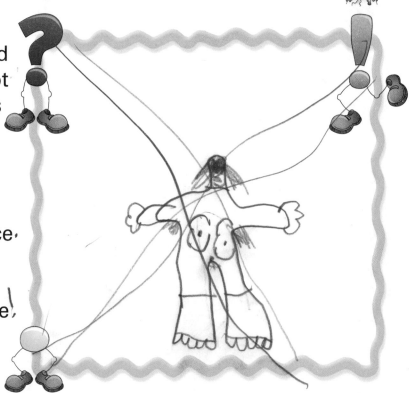

Match each pair of synonyms; then circle them in the puzzle.

Word List

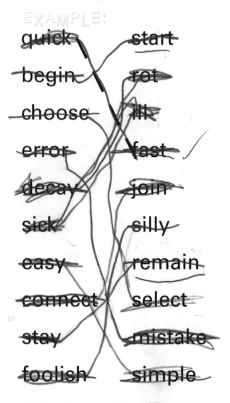

EXAMPLE:

quick	start
begin	rot
choose	ill
error	fast
decay	join
sick	silly
easy	remain
connect	select
stay	mistake
foolish	simple

a	b	c	z	o	w	r	y	m	p	d	e	f	h	j	k	m	o	s	i	c
e	a	s	y	a	d	f	l	d	e	c	a	y	r	b	m	b	d	k	r	o
o	p	s	q	u	i	c	k	q	r	s	r	t	u	e	v	w	x	y	z	n
b	z	i	o	e	v	f	u	v	w	x	o	z	e	g	d	f	k	l	k	n
c	d	m	n	o	p	a	a	p	y	t	t	o	u	i	k	l	a	c	b	e
d	k	p	w	x	z	s	y	p	q	x	a	u	t	n	s	t	a	r	t	c
o	u	l	o	o	i	t	a	d	f	f	e	s	e	l	e	c	t	o	e	t
z	a	e	m	n	o	p	q	r	s	o	t	u	v	r	w	x	c	y	z	j
k	i	e	r	r	o	r	s	t	u	o	p	k	d	e	b	a	h	i	u	o
l	o	m	i	s	t	a	k	e	z	l	u	p	i	m	g	h	o	k	o	i
m	u	g	j	l	p	q	g	r	s	i	v	w	u	a	z	g	o	i	l	n
i	p	b	d	f	g	l	i	o	z	s	s	p	o	i	u	i	s	g	o	m
l	z	w	x	y	z	u	g	a	b	h	d	l	e	n	i	u	e	o	b	c
l	s	i	c	k	p	s	i	l	l	y	m	u	s	t	a	y	y	i	o	e

Addition. Remember to add all three numbers.

2	4	5	9	7	4	5
3	4	1	1	2	0	5
+ 2	+ 2	+ 1	+ 0	+ 1	+ 4	+ 2
7 ✓	10 ✓	7 ✓	10 ✓	10 ✓	8 ✓	12 ✓

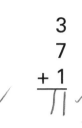

6	8	1	5	6	2	3
0	1	2	2	1	5	7
+ 2	+ 2	+ 6	+ 5	+ 7	+ 4	+ 1
8 ✓	11 ✓	9 ✓	12 ✓	14 ✓	11 ✓	11 ✓

2 + 2 + 2 = 6 ✓   0 + 0 + 8 = 8 ✓   1 + 0 + 8 = 9

5 + 1 + 1 = 7 ✓   2 + 5 + 3 = 10 ✓   9 + 2 + 2 = 13 ✓

3 + 2 + 3 = 8 ✓   2 + 3 + 4 = 9 ✓   4 + 5 + 1 = 10 ✓

When we add -ed or -d to a word, it shows something was done before. We usually use -d when the word ends in a vowel, and -ed when the word ends in a consonant. Look at the word, say the word, add -ed or -d to the word, and say the word again.

EXAMPLE:

wipe **d**   clean ed   rain ed

cook ed   walk ed   play ed

watch ed   work ed   talk ed

bath ed   wait ed   time ed

13

Read the sentence and underline the compound word. Then draw a line between the two words.

EXAMPLE:

1. Mary Ann lives on a house|boat.

2. My father won the down|hill race.

3. A rain|drop hit the white bunny on the nose.

4. Do you under|stand how to do this?

5. The fire|place was very dirty.

6. Did some|one ring your doorbell at 3 a.m.?

7. Pigs, horses, and cows are in the barn|yard.

8. I had to clean my bed|room this morning.

9. The snow|flakes fell very thick and heavy this winter.

Write the words in the correct ball.

EXAMPLE:

who
Tom
baby
Grandpa
_____

big truck
7:00 p.m.
outside
noon
Tom
under a tree
in my bed
tomorrow
Grandpa
jet
baby
book

what
big truck
jet
book
_____

where
under a tree
in my bed
outside
_____

when
7:00 p.m.
noon
tomorrow
_____

Place Value. Tell how many tens and ones.

EXAMPLE:

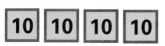 

tens	ones
4	5

_45_

tens	ones
3	5

_35_

dimes	pennies
4	4

_44_

dimes	pennies
2	5

_25_

_2_ tens _3_ ones = _23_

_3_ tens _0_ ones = _30_

Finish the story. Give it a title and draw a picture for it.

The Deadly Mountain

My friend, ___BOB___, and I
went for a hike in the mountains.
At a steep place on the path, we
slipped and fell into a hole. We
went down and down. We didn't
think we would ever stop falling.
When we hit the bottom of the
hole, we found...

a (dead) body, a spider
and a rat. $o one (police)
called the (polis)
and (thay) came
they

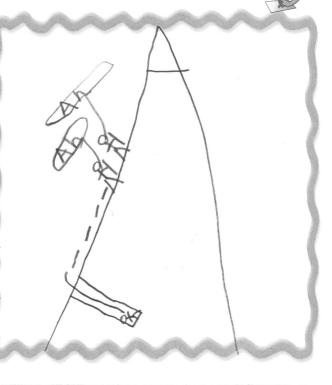

Circle the main idea of these stories.

I love books. In the summer I go to the library every other day. I check out books about horses and airplanes. I also like to read about football. I don't like how quiet I have to be in the library.

a. football books

b. at the library ✓

c. being quiet

Sometimes we have dreams that frighten us. Once, I dreamed I was falling over a cliff. I woke up shaking; I was so scared. My friend, Nan, dreamed a monster was coming after her. She hid in a big box so he couldn't find her. She woke up just as the monster put his hand in the box.

a. falling over a cliff

b. dreaming of monsters ✓

c. scary dreams

How many? Put an X on the line to answer each question.

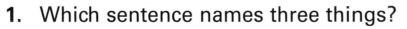

1. Which sentence names three things?

   __X__ Allie took a book, a bag, and an umbrella to school.

   _____ Allie took a bookbag and an umbrella to school.

2. Which sentence names four people?

   _____ Grayson, Mary Jane, and I went shopping.

   __X__ Grayson, Mary, Jane, and I went shopping.

3. Which sentence names two things?

   _____ Tanner put the lunch, box, and book on the table.

   __X__ Tanner put the lunchbox and book on the table.

Greater Than >, Less Than <. Put the correct sign in the circle.

2 < 4   19 < 91   14 > 4

9 < 10   64 > 46   29 < 30 ✓

16 < 20   32 > 23   71 > 18

124 < 216   592 > 324   2 + 4 > 1 + 4   5 + 4 > 8 − 2
                                                       9

322 > 100   985 > 850   9 − 2 < 6 + 2   3 − 2 < 5 − 2 ✓
                                7

648 < 846   745 < 746   4 + 4 > 1 + 4   7 − 3 > 1 + 2
                                8   5   4   3

Circle the correct numeral for each number word.

A. forty-five   **B.** eighty-one   **C.** three

54   (45)   18   (81)   30   (3)

D. fifty-eight   **E.** thirty   **F.** fifteen

(58)   85   (30)   31   (15)   50

Write the number words for the following numerals:
0, 20, 30, 40, 60, and 80.

zero   thirty   sixty

twenty   fourty   eighty

Read the stories. Circle the choice that tells what happens next.

1. Matt put his arms around the box. He could not lift it. He would need some help. The box was too heavy for him.

Matt will _____.

a. run outside and play
b. go ask his dad for help
c. hit the box with an ax
d. send the box to his friend

2. The children were playing outside. It started to get dark. They could see a flash of light and hear a loud sound. The wind began to blow.

"Let's go," shouted Ann. "It's ___."

a. time to eat
b. going to blow us away
c. going to rain soon
d. time for bed

3. Mary likes to ride her bike to school. One day she rode her bike over some glass.

The next day Mary walked to school because__.

a. she liked to walk
b. her bike had a flat tire
c. her brother rode her bike
d. her bike was red

Design and color your own T-shirt.
Write at least 10 words to describe it.

2 snakes, 2 people, 2 grows, 2 snakecatchers and a shirt.

Circle the shape that is on the bottom of the first shape in the row.

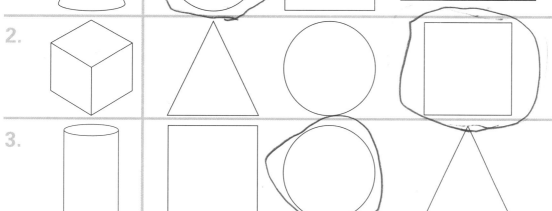

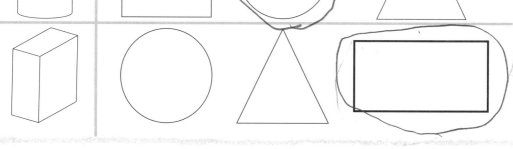

When we add **-ing** to a word, it shows that something is being done now. Look at the word, say the word, add **-ing** to the word, and say the word again.

go **ing**   say _ing_   do _ing_

sleep _ing_   walk _ing_   read _ing_

paint _ing_   work _ing_   eat _ing_

spell _ing_   cook _ing_   watch _ing_

Answer the questions.
Write complete sentences.

√ **1.** What do you use your ears for?

You use your ears for hearing.

√ **2.** What do zoo workers do for the animals?

Zoo workers feed them and take care of them.

3. What would you use to make a cage for a hamster?

I would use metal.

√ **4.** What are dogs, cats, cows, and deer?

They are all mamals.

√ **5.** How did you get to and from school last year?

My mom drove me.

Read and follow the directions carefully.

1. Make a box around all the animals.
2. Put a circle around all the tools.
3. Draw a line under all the things we wear.
4. Put a ⭐ on all the places in a house.
5. Write an **X** on all the noises.

crash   saw   hammer   bedroom

playroom   bang   kitchen   bear

yell   pants   fox   bathroom

whisper   rabbit   wrench   boom

closet   shoes   elephant   hat

shirt   hat   deer   can

Subtraction.

Subtract 6	
8	2
12	6
9	3
11	5
7	1
13	7

Subtract 8	
8	0
11	3
12	4
19	11
10	2
14	6

Subtract 7	
14	7
8	1
7	0
10	3
12	5
9	2

Look at the map and map key to answer the questions.

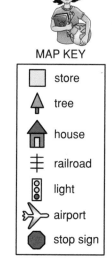

1. How many stores are there? __6__

2. What street has the most houses? _Oak_

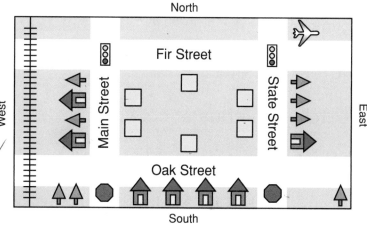

3. What two streets does the railroad go across?
   Oak street & _Fir street_

4. How many trees are west of the airport? __4__

5. What two streets have stop signs?
   Main Street & _State Street._

6. What three streets have traffic lights? __Fir__, __State__, & __Main__

Use the Table of Contents to answer the questions.

1. On what <u>page</u> could you <s>begin</s> reading about where ants live?

   ✗ ___4___ 5

2. In what <u>chapter</u> would you look to read about ant families?

   ✗ ✓ ___6___

3. On what page would you look to find the index?

   ✓ ✗ ___26___

4. What is the title of the first chapter?

   ___All about Ants___

Fill in the boxes with number words. Use some words more than once.

EXAMPLE:

1. Tanner wakes up at | s | e | v | e | n | o'clock.

2. He eats breakfast at | s | e | v | e | n | o'clock.

3. Tanner catches the bus at | e | i | g | h | t | thirty.

4. School starts at | n | i | n | e | o'clock.

5. Recess is at | t | e | n | o'clock in the morning and | o | n | e | o'clock in the afternoon.

6. Tanner eats lunch at | t | w | e | l | v | e | o'clock.

7. School is out at | t | h | r | e | e | thirty. ✓

8. Tanner eats dinner at | f | i | v | e | o'clock.

9. He plays until bedtime at | e | i | g | h | t | o'clock.

Write the number by the word.

forty	40	eight	8	one	1
sixteen	16	seventeen	17	eighteen	18
four	4	fifty	50	thirty	30

nine	9	two	2	ninety-nine	99
twelve	12	nineteen	19	seven	7
ten	10	eleven	11	thirteen	13
fifteen	5	thirty-three	33	fourteen	14

Write five words that rhyme with each key word.

abcdefghijklm nopqrstuvwxyz

EXAMPLE:

sack
back
tack
wack
smack
stack
snack

rock
dock
shock
stock
lock
clock

deck
heck
neck
peck
wreck
tech

lick
nick
stick
flick
kick
pick

queen
lean
seen
bean
mean
green

king
ding
fling
swing
bling
sting

song
strong
wrong
dong
long
pong

rung
strung
flung
hung
sung
tongue

Tell what or whom the words mean.

FACTOID
The military salute came from knights raising their visors to the king.

EXAMPLE: The boys ran away.
They ran to school. They = **boys**

1. Carla and I like horses. We ride them every day.
   them = horses

2. Grandma called today. She is coming to see us.
   She = Grandma

3. Joe would like to fly in a jet. He has never been in one.
   He = Joe   one = jet

4. This summer, I am at camp. I like it here.
   here = camp

5. I lost my best umbrella. It is blue.
   It = umbrella

6. Lee has two dogs. They are both black.
   They = dogs

**Read each sentence. Look carefully at the underlined word.
Is it spelled right or wrong? Mark your answer.**

		Right	**Wrong**
EXAMPLE:			
1.	Randy ate toast with jam on it.	●	○
2.	We wunt to the store for some candy.	○	◉
3.	The dog will hund for his bone.	○	◉
4.	We will plant our garden tonight.	◉	○
5.	The keng asked the queen to come quickly.	○	◉
6.	This is the ent of my story.	○	◉
7.	I want my hair to grow very long.	◉	○
8.	Think of a good name for a pet.	◉	○

What does the circled digit mean? Circle the answer.
Be sure to read the words.

EXAMPLE:

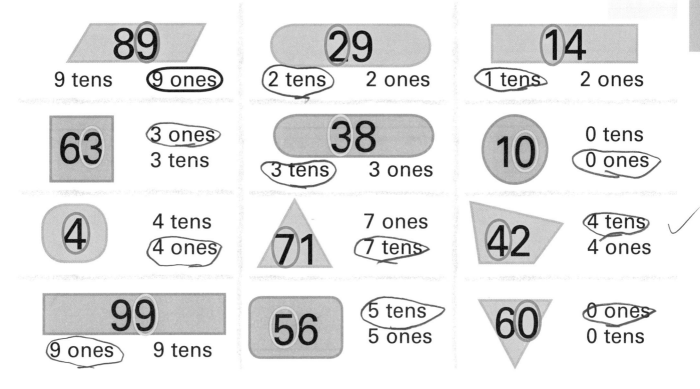

89 — 9 tens — (9 ones)

29 — (2 tens) — 2 ones

14 — (1 tens) — 2 ones

63 — (3 ones) — 3 tens

38 — (3 tens) — 3 ones

10 — 0 tens — (0 ones)

4 — 4 tens — (4 ones)

71 — 7 ones — (7 tens)

42 — (4 tens) ✓ — 4 ones

99 — (9 ones) — 9 tens

56 — (5 tens) — 5 ones

60 — (0 ones) — 0 tens

Story Titles. Rule: The first and all other important words in a story or book title begin with a capital letter. Write these story titles correctly.

EXAMPLE:

1. an exciting camping trip _____ **An Exciting Camping Trip**

2. my ride on an elephant _____ My Ride On An Elephant ✓

3. the day we missed school _____ The Day We Missed school

4. pets are fun _____ Pets Are Fun

5. a real fire drill _____ A Real Fire Drill

6. my vacation this summer _____ My Vacation This Summer

Study the pictograph. Read each question and circle your answer. The first one is done for you.

Number of flowers picked. Each 🌼 = 2 flowers

Allie 🌼 🌼 🌼

Sue 🌼 🌼 🌼 🌼 🌼

Denise 🌼 🌼

Beth 🌼 🌼 🌼 🌼 🌼 🌼

Lori 🌼 🌼 🌼 🌼 🌼

1. What did these girls pick?
   a. trees　(b. flowers)　c. weeds

2. How many flowers does 🌼 stand for?
   a. one　(b. two)　c. three

3. How many flowers did Allie and Denise pick together?
   a. two　c. eight
   (b. ten)　d. five

4. Who picked the most flowers?
   a. Allie　c. Sue　e. Denise
   (b. Beth)　d. Lori

5. Which two girls picked the same number of flowers?
   (a. Sue & Lori)　c. Allie & Lori
   b. Sue & Beth　d. Denise & Allie

6. Who picked the least?
   a. Allie　(b. Denise)
   How many did she pick?
   a. eight　b. two　(c. four)

7. Who picked six flowers?
   a. Denise　b. Sue　(c. Allie)

Write a dinner menu for a dragon! Draw a picture to go with it!

DRAGON DINNER MENU
great whight
shark fillet
Perana soop
fireball cake
Pickeld eyeball
saled terantala
pizza, tounge
stew

Love It!

Read the story. Write the problem and the answer.

EXAMPLE:

1. Tanner had 8 balls.
He lost 2 of them.
How many balls does he
have now?

___**8 – 2**___ = __6__ balls

2. Allie has 4 dolls.
She got 6 more for
her birthday. How many
dolls does Allie have?

__4 + 6__ = _10_ dolls ✓

3. We had 11 goldfish. Our
cat ate 9 of them. How
many goldfish were not
eaten?

__11 – 9__ = _2_ goldfish ✓

4. Rob walked 3 miles, Lori
walked 6 miles, and Matt
walked 4 miles. How many
miles did the children walk
in all?

__3+6+4__ = _13_ miles ✓

5. Matt has two dogs, Tina
and Joy. Tina had 8 pup-
pies, and Joy had 4. How
many puppies are there in
all?

__8+4__ = _12_ puppies ✓

6. I bought one dozen eggs
(12). On the way home
from the store, I broke 5 of
them. How many eggs did
not get broken?

__12 – 5__ = _7_ eggs ✓

**Circle and write the correct word for each sentence. Remember: When
you add -s or -es to a word, it means more than one.**

1. Two _girls_ went for a ride. **girl**   ~~girls~~

2. My _dish_ broke when it fell. ~~dish~~   **dishes**

3. Which _pencil_ is yours? ~~pencil~~   **pencils**

4. Put all the _books_ back on the shelf. **book**   ~~books~~ ✓

5. My foot is nine _inches_ long. **inch**   ~~inches~~

6. How many _boats_ were in the race? **boat**   ~~boats~~

7. May I have a piece of _pie_ ? ~~pie~~   **pies**

8. Where are my _shoes_? **shoe**   ~~shoes~~

What does the underlined word mean? Circle your answer.

FACTOID
Butterflies taste their food with their feet.

1. She has on a <u>dark</u> purple dress.
   a. not light   **b.** night

2. We were <u>safe</u> on the rock.
   a. without danger
   b. place to keep things

3. Sam had to be home before <u>dark</u>.
   a. night   **b.** morning   **c.** day

4. Can you <u>lift</u> this box?
   a. pick up   **b.** put down   **c.** turn over

5. I need <u>several</u> people to help me.
   a. none   **b.** one   **c.** some   **d.** hundreds

Fill in the banks with <u>str-</u>, <u>spr-</u>, <u>spl-</u>, or <u>thr-</u>; then follow the directions at the bottom of the page.

___ ___ ___ **ead**	___ ___ ___ **eet**	___ ___ ___ **ang**
___ ___ ___ **it**	___ ___ ___ **ong**	___ ___ ___ **ay**
___ ___ ___ **ough**	___ ___ ___ **ash**	___ ___ ___ **ow**
___ ___ ___ **ee**	___ ___ ___ **ing**	___ ___ ___ **atter**

1. Color the **spr-** words yellow.
2. Put an **X** on the **spl-** words.

3. Circle the **thr-** words.
4. Color the **str-** words orange.

Write the missing sign (+, −, or =) in the circle.

6 ◯ 3 = 9   12 ◯ 6 = 6   4 ◯ 2 = 2

4 + 3 ◯ 7   14 ◯ 1 = 15   12 ◯ 2 = 10

9 ◯ 3 = 6   14 ◯ 4 = 10   14 − 7 ◯ 7

4 ◯ 1 = 3   7 − 3 ◯ 4   3 ◯ 3 = 6

8 ◯ 4 = 12   9 ◯ 2 = 11   11 ◯ 2 = 9

7 + 3 ◯ 10   10 ◯ 3 = 13   12 − 4 ◯ 8

10 ◯ 8 = 2   3 ◯ 8 = 11   10 + 2 ◯ 12

4 ◯ 4 = 8   6 + 4 ◯ 10   0 + 9 ◯ 9

Look at each base word and add the endings -er and -est.

	-er	-est
thin	**thinner**	**thinnest**
slim	_____	_____
big	_____	_____
hot	_____	_____
red	_____	_____

Write the correct ending on each base word in the sentence.

1. That's the big_____ cake on the table.

2. My cheeks are red_____ than your coat.

3. Jenna is slim_____ than her brother.

4. Today is the hot_____ day we have had so far.

5. My sandwich is thin_____ than yours.

Fill in the blanks. Use the words under the sentences.

1. We dressed in special _____ for the party.
   cloth   **clothes**   **clothed**

2. She turned on the _____ as we came in the room.
   light   **lighted**   **lighting**

3. We take our _____ when we go camping.
   lately   **tent**   **rain**

4. We had _____ for dinner.
   banks   **beaned**   **beans**

5. My bedroom is _____.
   blow   **blew**   **blue**

Look at the index below from the back of a book about flowers. Write the page where you could find information on each of the following flowers.

1. tulips _____

2. pansies _____

3. daisies _____

4. roses _____

5. zinnia _____

6. lily _____

Fill in the missing numbers.

| 300 | | 302 | | | 305 | | | 309 |

| | 311 | | | | 316 | | |

| 489 | | 491 | | | 495 | | |

| 202 | | | | | | | 210 |

| 595 | | 597 | | | 601 | | |

Circle the words that should have a capital letter. Put a period (.) or question mark (?) at the end of each sentence.

EXAMPLE:

1. (rachel) lives in (new) (york) (city) • ___
2. i live in salt lake city, utah ___
3. where do you live ___
4. mr. brown is my best neighbor ___
5. was easter in april this year ___
6. my mother shops at smith's market ___
7. where is dallas, texas ___
8. look what i've got ___
9. children say "trick or treat" on halloween ___
10. do you like christmas or thanksgiving better ___

Fill in the blanks. Use the words in the box.

trade	summer	cowboy
dry	ambulance	brought

1. Do you like to go swimming in the _____?

2. My little brother wants to be a _____ when he grows up.

3. The _____ made a loud noise as it passed us.

4. I'll _____ my banana for your orange.

5. Sammy _____ a big snake to school in a box.

6. The ground has not been _____ this summer.

Use the dictionary entry below to answer the questions.

germ (jûrm), n. 1. disease-producing microbe. 2. a bud or seed.

1. What part of speech is germ? _____

2. Which definition of germ deals with growing plants?

   _____

3. Would the word germinate come before or after the word germ in the dictionary? _____

4. Use the word germ in a sentence.

   _____

The Impossible Balloon

Air is all around us, taking up lots of space. This may be hard to imagine since you can't really see air or feel anything solid when you reach out to touch it. Try this activity, and you'll see just how pushy air can be!

Stuff You Need:

balloon
soda bottle (2-liter)

Here's What to Do:

1. Take your balloon and put it inside the bottle. Be careful not to drop it in the bottle. Hold on to the mouth of the balloon and pull it back over the mouth of the bottle so that it stays in place.

2. Put your lips on the bottle. Try to blow up the balloon.

What's This All About?

When the balloon is wrapped around the mouth of the bottle, it seals the bottle. No air can get in or out of the bottle. As you try to blow up the balloon, it pushes against the air trapped inside the bottle. The air does not like this, so it pushes back on the balloon, refusing to let it get any bigger. Air takes up space and can push back on things that push on it.

More Fun Ideas to Try:

1. Try different sizes of bottles to see if you can blow up the balloon in a bigger bottle.

2. Try round balloons or long balloons to see if that makes a difference. Write down what you think might happen before you try the experiment.

3. Try a plastic bottle with a small hole punched in the bottom and see if you can blow up the balloon.

Napkin Preserver

Do you believe it's possible to dunk a napkin in an aquarium and have it be dry when you pull it out? See if your napkin "sinks or swims" while proving that air takes up space!

Stuff You Need:

aquarium or large, clear container
drinking glass (any size)
napkin
water

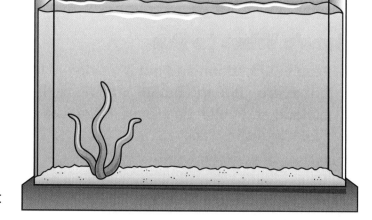

Here's What to Do:

1. Make sure the napkin is dry.

2. Stuff the napkin into the bottom of the glass. Turn the glass upside down over the floor to make sure the napkin won't fall out.

3. Keep the glass upside down and slowly lower it straight into the aquarium until the napkin and glass are both completely underwater. Don't tilt the glass at all. Now, remove the glass from the water.

4. Look at the napkin closely. Is it still dry?

What's This All About?

This activity shows that air certainly does take up space. As the glass is lowered into the container, the air inside the glass displaces (or pushes away) the water in the container. Because the water is displaced, the napkin remains dry. Pretty cool, huh?

More Fun Ideas to Try:

If you are having a hard time seeing how air takes up space, just put your hands on your chest, fingers spread. Inhale, hold your breath, and then exhale. Can you see now how air takes up space?

Motivational Calendar

Month

My parents and I decided that if I complete
20 days of **Summer Bridge Activities**™ and
read _____ minutes a day, my incentive/reward will be:

Child's Signature _____ Parent's Signature_____

Day 1	☆	📖	_____	Day 11	☆	📖	_____
Day 2	☆	📖	_____	Day 12	☆	📖	_____
Day 3	☆	📖	_____	Day 13	☆	📖	_____
Day 4	☆	📖	_____	Day 14	☆	📖	_____
Day 5	☆	📖	_____	Day 15	☆	📖	_____
Day 6	☆	📖	_____	Day 16	☆	📖	_____
Day 7	☆	📖	_____	Day 17	☆	📖	_____
Day 8	☆	📖	_____	Day 18	☆	📖	_____
Day 9	☆	📖	_____	Day 19	☆	📖	_____
Day 10	☆	📖	_____	Day 20	☆	📖	_____

Child: Color the ☆ for daily activities completed.
Color the 📖 for daily reading completed.

Parent: Initial the ____ when all activities are complete.

Discover Something New!

Fun Activity Ideas to Go Along with the Second Section!

1. Have a contest to name the state capitals.

2. Find out what causes hiccups.

3. Watch a science program on TV.

4. Make dessert tonight.

5. Plan a hike at a nearby canyon.

6. Weed your garden.

7. Visit a historical site.

8. Do chalk art on the front sidewalk.

9. Play a game involving math, like Racko, Uno, or Monopoly.

10. Paint a picture with lemon juice on white paper—hang it in a sunny window. See what happens in a few days.

11. Make a list of environmental problems. Decide how to help by changing things in your home (collecting aluminum cans, etc.).

12. Go on a penny walk. On each corner, flip a penny to decide which way to go.

13. Have each family member write another family member a thank-you note.

14. Cover a table in the yard with paper and paint a picture using pudding.

15. Make a date with your parents to attend a musical event.

16. Hide "I love you" notes under your parents' pillows.

17. Do a pioneer activity. Brainstorm and be creative.

18. Take a counting walk: how many steps to the mailbox, how many to a friend's house, etc.

19. Give your pet a party. Invite its friends.

20. Parents' Day (new holiday). Take 'em breakfast in bed.

Build the pyramid. Write the answers in the stones.

EXAMPLE:

| 3 | +1 | 4 | −1 | 3 | +2 | 5 |

| 5 | −2 | | +4 | | −2 | | +4 | | −4 | 5 |

| 9 | −6 | | −3 | | +8 | | +2 | | −7 | 3 |

| 12 | −8 | | +6 | | −4 | | −2 | | +9 | | +2 | | −5 | 10 |

Some words end with two of the same consonant.

| off | fell | dress | stiff | shall |
| class | stuff | glass | ball | mitt | hill |

1. Write the word from the box that rhymes with these words.

bell _____

fill _____

puff _____

_____

_____

_____

2. Fill in the missing word or words. Use words from the box.

Our _____ will put on a play for you.

I _____ down and hurt my hand.

Put some milk in my _____, please.

Grab your _____, and let's play _____.

The man is on top of the _____.

Stand still, and I will show you my new _____.

Could It Really Happen? Read the sentences. Write <u>yes</u> if what the sentence says could really happen. Write <u>no</u> if what the sentence says could not really happen.

1. Jennifer wears a watch on her nose. _____

2. A robin flew to its nest in the tree. _____

3. Robert helped his father paint the fence. _____

4. Paul saw a striped cat swim across the river. _____

5. Mandy eats her lunch with a hammer and saw. _____

6. We built a tunnel out of clay and rocks. _____

7. Birds use their beaks to fly. _____

8. Andy lost his tooth last night. _____

9. That cow is driving a bus! _____

10. The moose gave the frog a cookie. _____

Maps are fun. Use the map to complete the sentences.

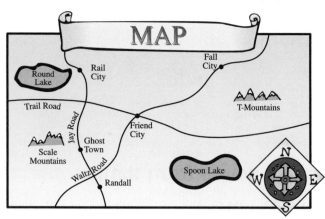

1. _____ Road runs north and south.

2. _____ Lake is between Trail Road and Jay Road.

3. _____ Mountains are the mountains in the south.

4. _____ Mountains are the mountains to the north.

5. _____ Road has the most cities on it.

6. _____ Town sounds spooky, _____ City sounds friendly, and _____ City sounds like you need to watch where you are going.

Add or subtract.

84	37	69	18	57	70	87
− 42	− 13	+ 20	− 4	+ 21	+ 30	− 36

22	24	10	23	26	35	99
− 16	− 11	− 10	+ 12	+ 22	+ 33	− 34

43	91	15	12	49	16	287
+ 43	+ 6	− 9	+ 2	− 38	+ 3	− 12

Read the words in each group and put them in the correct order.
Place a period (.) or a question mark (?) at the end of each sentence.
Read your sentence.

EXAMPLE:

__1__ It is fun   _____ Allie went   _____ bones

__3__ new friends.   _____ know where   _____ My dog

__2__ to make   _____ Do you   _____ can eat

_____ Ms. Hansen gave   _____ car passed   _____ Tanner are

_____ their papers   _____ A green   _____ Grayson and

_____ the children   _____ us   _____ brothers

_____ Matt has   _____ kinds of cookies   _____ love me

_____ of cars   _____ Denise ate   _____ and mom

_____ four kinds   _____ four different   _____ My dad

Read this paragraph; then follow the directions.

Denise likes to do many different things in the summer. Denise likes to sleep until eight o'clock. After she gets up, she likes to help her mother work in the garden for a while. Every day Denise likes to read and play with her friends. She likes to go swimming and hiking with her brothers. And most of all, she likes to ride her horse.

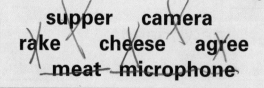

1. Underline the topic sentence.
2. Whom does Denise go swimming with? Circle your answer.
3. Put an **X** on the time Denise gets up.
4. What do you think would be a good name for Denise's horse?
   I would name it BoB!
5. Name two things that might be growing in Denise's garden.
   I think she will grow mushrooms.

Crossword Puzzle. Read the sentences. Choose a word from the box below to complete the puzzle.

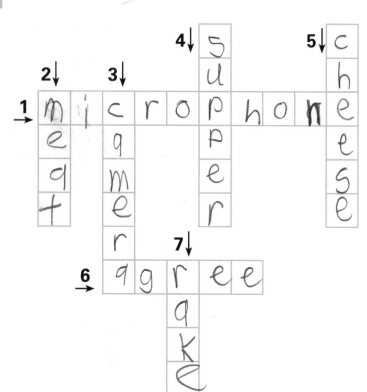

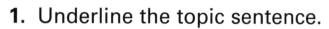

supper   camera
rake   cheese   agree
meat   microphone

1. You talk into this to make your voice loud.
2. You can eat this.
3. You take pictures with this.
4. You eat this at night.
5. People and mice like this.
6. My friend and I _____ on most things.
7. You do this to the leaves on your lawn.

Connect the dots. Start with 597.

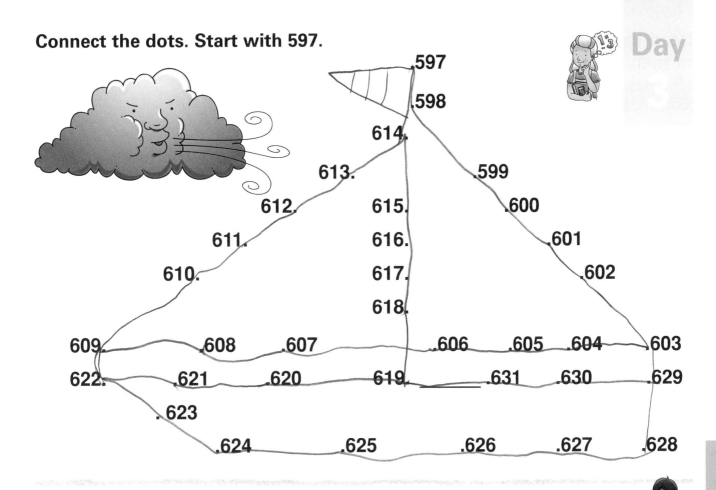

Choose the correct word from the box to complete the sentence.

1. The train will _stop_ .
   The train is _stoping_ .
   The train has _stoped_ .

1.	stopped
	~~stopping~~
	~~stop~~

2. The baby can _clap_ .
   See, the baby is _clapping_ .
   The baby _clapped_ .

2.	~~clap~~
	~~clapped~~
	~~clapping~~

3. The rabbit is _hopping_ .
   The rabbit _hopped_ .
   The rabbit can _hop_ .

3.	~~hop~~
	~~hopped~~
	~~hopping~~

4. Let's play _tag_ .
   I'm _taging_ you.
   I _tagged_ John.

4.	~~tagged~~
	tagging
	~~tag~~

Read the words in the box. Choose five of them and write your own sentences. Use capital letters, periods, question marks, and exclamation points.

career	adult	complete	prepare
stranger	interested	college	during

1. _____

2. _____

3. _____

4. _____

Circle the one that holds the most.

1. Tablespoon   Teaspoon   1/2 Teaspoon

2. QUART Milk   One Gallon Milk   2 QUARTS Milk

3. Orange Juice   (bottle)   2 QUARTS Orange Juice

4. (measuring cup)   (measuring cup)   (measuring cup)

Write the number fact families.

EXAMPLE:

1.

(11
6   5)

_6_ + _5_ = _11_
_5_ + _6_ = _11_
_11_ − _5_ = _6_
_11_ − _6_ = _5_

2.

(4
5   9)

____ + ____ = ____
____ + ____ = ____
____ − ____ = ____
____ − ____ = ____

3.

(7
5   12)

____ + ____ = ____
____ + ____ = ____
____ − ____ = ____
____ − ____ = ____

Read the words. Print the soft c words in the celery. Print the hard c words in the carrot.

cat	~~celery~~	once	rascal	excited	scene
cider	come	century	factor	dance	~~carrot~~
city	candy	actor	raccoon	magic	sentence

soft c = s sound
celery _____ _____ _____
_____ _____ _____

hard c = k sound
carrot _____ _____
_____ _____ _____
_____ _____ _____

Write the correct contraction for each sentence.

FACTOID
Almonds are in the same family as peaches.

EXAMPLE:

1. _____**They've**_____ never played football.
   They're   They'll   They've

2. _____ have a really fun time.
   We're   We'll   We've

3. _____ work as hard as I can.
   I'm   I've   I'll

4. _____ got to do it right the first time.
   We've   We'll   We're

5. _____ all in this together.
   We'll   We're   We've

6. _____ not going to run away with it.
   They'll   They've   They're

Write the picture's number by its description.

1.

2.

3.

4.

____2____ keeps you dry when it rains

_____ a vegetable rabbits like

_____ a place to sleep

_____ use this to get clean

_____ hurts your teeth

_____ a red fruit

_____ cats and kittens like to drink this

_____ time to get up

5.

6.

7.

8.

Match the problems that have the same sum.

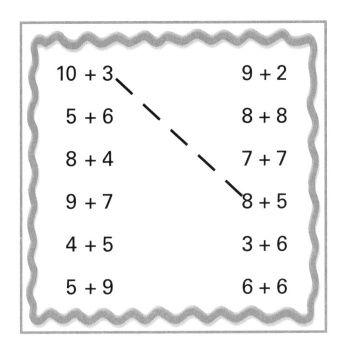

10 + 3	9 + 2
5 + 6	8 + 8
8 + 4	7 + 7
9 + 7	8 + 5
4 + 5	3 + 6
5 + 9	6 + 6

4 + 6	4 + 2
6 + 9	5 + 13
9 + 8	8 + 2
6 + 0	3 + 9
9 + 9	7 + 8
7 + 5	14 + 3

Answer the questions below and complete the calendar.

1. Starting on the proper day of the week for this year, write in the numbers for each day of July.
2. July always has _____ days.
3. Which day of the week is Independence Day? _____
4. July comes in what season? _____
5. How many Saturdays are in July? _____
6. Draw a flag on the Fourth of July.

 July

Year_____

Sunday	Monday	Tuesday	Wednesday	Thursday	Friday	Saturday

Read the stories. Decide what will happen next. Underline your answer.

FACTOID
Do you know how to tell if a cranberry is ripe? If it bounces well!

1. Lori was about to take a big bite out of her ice cream. Denise bumped her arm. What will happen next?

Lori will drink some milk.
Lori will yell at Denise.
Lori will get ice cream on her shorts.

2. Matt was playing tennis with Grayson. The sun was very hot. The boys' faces were getting too much sun. What will happen next?

Grayson and Matt will get sunburned.
Matt will go home.
Matt and Grayson will get cold.

Look at the pictures. Read the sentences below. Write the sentence number in the box of the matching picture.

☐    ☐    ☐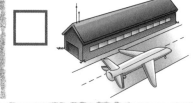

☐    ☐    ☐

1. I am very hot and dry. Sometimes in the spring I have flowers.

2. People can go anywhere if they come to me first.

3. Here you can see many animals and people doing fun things.

4. You come to me on some days and learn.

5. This is something that every living thing needs.

6. I am a very special day in July.

Subtract.

1. 14   11   15   16   14   12   13
    − 5   − 4   − 6   − 8   − 7   − 7   − 5

2. 17   15   18   14   12   16   11
    − 9   − 8   − 9   − 6   − 4   − 5   − 6

Use the words <u>who</u>, <u>what</u>, <u>when</u>, <u>why</u>, and <u>where</u> in the blanks to complete the sentences below.

1. _____ will it be time to leave?

2. _____ wants to come with me?

3. _____ didn't you do your work?

4. _____ shall we go after the movie?

5. _____ time did you say it was?

6. _____ did you put my shoes and socks?

7. _____ must you leave so soon?

8. _____ are you doing now?

Use the words <u>went</u> or <u>gone</u> to finish these sentences. **Remember:** The word <u>gone</u> needs another word to help it, such as <u>has</u> or <u>have</u>.

FACTOID
Birds could never be astronauts. They need gravity to swallow!

EXAMPLE:

1. Tanner _____**went**_____ home after school.

2. Grayson has _____ shopping for a new coat.

3. Matt _____ with Denise to play.

4. We have _____ with Matt's mother all week.

5. Mother _____ to work this morning.

6. Allie has _____ around the corner.

7. Who has _____ on a trip before?

8. My aunt _____ skating on the ice.

9. I have _____ to bed.

10. He _____ around the world in an airplane.

At the top of each page in a dictionary are guide words. The guide word on the left tells you the first word found on the page. The guide word on the right tells you the last word on the page. Circle the word that would be found on the page with the following guide words.

1. **patter—penguin**

   panda   pig   paw

2. **match—monkey**

   moan   magic   motor

3. **alligator—anteater**

   antelope   animal   antler

4. **bear—buffalo**

   bunny   bat   bison

Circle the time that matches the clock.

10:15   8:10   9:15

8:30   12:45   1:45

6:00   12:00   12:30

8:25   6:25   5:08

5:30   6:40   5:40

1:05   12:00   12:05

Make one dollar in change in six different combinations.

EXAMPLE:

quarters ___2___
dimes ___4___
nickels ___2___
pennies ___0___
Total $ __1.00__

quarters _____
dimes _____
nickels _____
pennies _____
Total $_____

quarters _____
dimes _____
nickels _____
pennies _____
Total $_____

quarters _____
dimes _____
nickels _____
pennies _____
Total $_____

quarters _____
dimes _____
nickels _____
pennies _____
Total $_____

quarters _____
dimes _____
nickels _____
pennies _____
Total $_____

Ask someone to say one of the words in each box. Circle the word they say. When you finish, read all of the words on the page out loud.

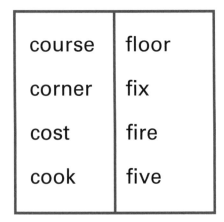

course	floor
corner	fix
cost	fire
cook	five

instead	east
inside	else
into	easy
income	engine

begin	point
behind	plane
began	pickle
before	push

until	throw
unusually	through
unlace	those
unit	that

alarm	weather
adjust	wagon
alone	weave
afraid	weep

shape	year
snake	young
stone	yeast
stopped	yell

Unscramble and write the missing words.

1. My mom always _____ me when I go to _____.
   ghus   **dbe**

2. Rob says that he _____ go home _____.
   sutm   **won**

3. The _____ swam in the _____ water.
   shif   **eedp**

4. My dad has to _____ our grass; it's too _____.
   tcu   **glno**

5. The cat chased _____ the mouse in his _____.
   frate   **ouhse**

6. Lori walks home from _____, and Matt _____.
   schloo   **diers**

Add the ones first and then the tens.

Day

|1| □ □ □ □ □
63 47 19 55 24 88
+8 +8 +8 +9 +7 +6
71

□ □ □ □ □ □
63 72 48 37 27 16
+9 +8 +4 +5 +6 +6

□ □ □ □ □ □
4 33 47 19 28 8
+16 +8 +7 +9 +7 +42

Sounds: (o͞o) (o͝o). Circle the words that have the o͞o sound, like <u>tooth</u>, in green. Circle the words that have the o͝o sound, like <u>hook</u>, in blue.

hood

book

cookies

boot   cool   booth

moon   brook

spoon   goose

school   crook

moose   hoop   stool

soon   tooth

scoop   cook

tool   balloon

foot   stood

food   broom

took

zoo   wood

wool   look

pool

Read the story about Max and Joy. Write an <u>M</u> by the phrases that describe Max and a <u>J</u> by the phrases that describe Joy. Write a <u>B</u> if the phrase describes both of them.

Max and Joy are twins. They have brown eyes and black hair. They are seven years old and go to school. Max likes math, and Joy likes to read. They both like to go outside to play. Joy likes to play ball. Max likes to run and play tag. Joy likes to ride her bike while Max feeds his pet dog.

____ **1.** has brown eyes   ____ **2.** are twins

____ **3.** likes to read   ____ **4.** are seven

____ **5.** likes to ride bikes   ____ **6.** likes to run

____ **7.** likes to play ball   ____ **8.** likes math

____ **9.** has a pet   ____ **10.** has black hair

Matter is all around us. It can be solid like wood, liquid like milk, or gas like steam. Unscramble the words and fill in the blanks.

1. Ice is a _____. When it melts, it is a _____.
   dliso   **ildqui**

2. I have no shape. You can feel me when the wind blows. _____.
   asg

3. Matter is what things are made of.
   It has three forms: _____, _____, and _____.
   sga   **dqiiul**   **osdil**

4. _____ can be big or little, soft or hard.
   tertaM

5. _____ takes the shape of what you put it in.
   qidiLu

6. Rocks are _____.
   odlsi

7. You can take a bath in this matter: _____.
   ilqidu

8. Air is a _____.
   sag

Count the money. Color the item that costs more.

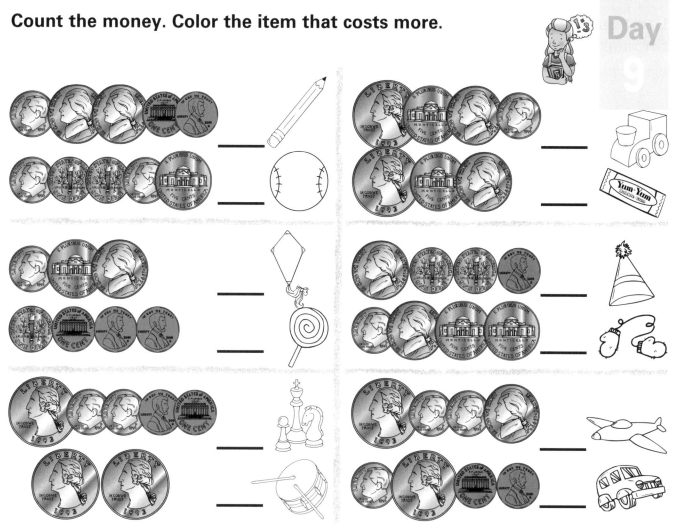

Listen to the vowel sounds. If the word has a short vowel sound, put an <u>S</u> on the line. If the vowel sound is long, put an <u>L</u> on the line.

EXAMPLE:

just	**S**	clock ____	name ____
cute	**L**	slow ____	truck ____
nice ____		cape ____	help ____
road ____		clue ____	chip ____
ship ____		apple ____	trike ____
shot ____		seed ____	shame ____
left ____		gum ____	goat ____
slam ____		sweet____	read ____

Can you find the answers to these puzzles? Choose a word from the box below.

dew   giraffe   crib   skunk   mouse   rope   glue   moose   broom

1. Cleo is black and white. He can make a terrible smell.

Cleo is a _____.

2. Sweep the floor with me.

I'm a _____.

3. Rick is small and gray. He has a long tail. He likes cheese.

Rick is a _____.

4. Tiny has a long neck and brown spots on her body. She eats leaves off the trees.

Tiny is a _____.

5. You can stick things together with me.

I am _____.

6. You can tie things up with me. I can be thick or thin.

I'm a _____.

7. Harry lives in the forest by a pond. He eats grass on the bottom of the pond and has big antlers.

Harry is a _____.

8. You can find me on the grass in the morning on cool days.

I am _____.

9. Babies sleep in me. I have four legs, but I can't walk.

I'm a _____.

Read the sentences and put an X on which happened first.

_____ I planted seeds.
_____ The flowers grew.

_____ I did my work.
_____ I must do my work.

_____ Katie spent all of her money.
_____ Katie has a lot of money.

_____ Kirt starts his car.
_____ Kirt drives his car.

_____ I brushed my teeth.
_____ I put toothpaste on my brush.

_____ Our snowman is tall.
_____ Our snowman melted.

_____ I put my shoes on.
_____ I put on my socks.

_____ Mom baked a cake.
_____ I ate a piece of cake.

Add.

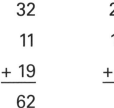

1					
32	28	70	44	57	26
11	14	99	2	32	33
+ 19	+ 4	+ 12	+ 38	+ 89	+ 44
62					

81	22	67	81	74	6
38	9	45	8	33	24
+ 64	+ 19	+ 15	+ 8	+ 17	+ 36

Put these words in alphabetical order. They are <u>r</u>-controlled vowel words. Can you spell them all?

her	card	jerk	turn	march
word	are	burn	more	store
bird	third	dark	part	first

1. _____   6. _____   11. _____

2. _____   7. _____   12. _____

3. _____   8. _____   13. _____

4. _____   9. _____   14. _____

5. _____   10. _____   15. _____

The syllables <u>be</u>, <u>a</u>, <u>re</u>, <u>ex</u>, and <u>de</u> are common beginning syllables. Read the words in each box. Circle the syllable common to each word. Then write the correct word in the blank. The first one has been done for you.

ⓐfraid	ⓐlive	ⓐhead
remove	repair	renew
exchange	exhibit	exit
before	because	became
about	around	alarming
decoy	decline	decree
receive	recall	recess
behind	belief	belong

1. I will walk ___ahead___ of you.

2. Will you please _____ my shoes?

3. Mom will _____ this dress for a skirt.

4. After ten years of school, my sister _____ a doctor.

5. This story was _____ some strange animals.

6. The king sent a _____ from the palace.

7. The children like _____ time.

8. I _____ to the school chorus.

Write a story called "My Favorite Month of the Year."

_____

_____

_____

_____

_____

_____

Write each problem; then solve it.

1. Lori has 13 pretty roses. She sold 9 of them. How many roses does she have left to sell?

_____ = _____ roses

2. Grayson can walk 2 miles in one hour. How many miles can he walk in two hours?

_____ = _____ miles

3. Matt has 14 toy cars, and Tanner has 10 toy cars. How many more cars does Matt have than Tanner?

_____ = _____ cars

4. Twenty-eight tigers were in a tent. Twenty-one went outside. How many stayed in the tent?

_____ = _____ tigers

5. Denise has 9 teddy bears. Allie has 6 dolls, and Lori has 3 balls. How many toys do the girls have in all?

_____ = _____ toys

The letters ph make the sound of (f)! Read the sentences and choose the correct word from the Word Box to fill in the blanks.

1. What is your _____ number?

2. We saw _____ at the zoo.

3. Allie wrote the letters of the _____.

4. Our team will get a _____.

5. Andy is my neat _____.

6. Lori likes to sing into the _____.

Word Box

trophy

phone

alphabet

elephants

microphone

nephew

Compound Words. Choose the right word for each sentence.

1. Denise is one of my favorite _____.
   classmates   rainbows   buttermilk

2. Allie likes to go _____ in the sand.
   footstool   barefoot   football

3. It rains a lot during _____.
   summertime   springtime   lunchtime

4. Put the _____ on to set the table.
   tablecloth   washcloth   pitchfork

5. Our family ate crab at _____.
   dinnertime   snowflake   shoelace

6. I like to collect _____ at the beach.
   storybooks   seashells   butterflies

Draw a line from the word in the first column to the words that best describe it.

EXAMPLE:

1. milk ————————————— a farm animal

2. ice cream ————————— something to drink

3. dog   a special planet

4. cow   usually very cold

5. yellow   a type of tent

6. hammer   a pet

7. Earth   a color

8. teepee   a tool

Write the temperature in the first blank. Write <u>warm</u> or <u>cold</u> in the second blank.

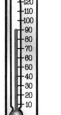 

1. _____ ° F

_____

2. _____ ° F

_____

3. _____ ° F

_____

4. _____ ° F

_____

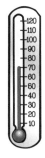

Put the words from the box below into the correct categories.

cow	blocks	rabbit	beans	bread	monkey
ball	sled	kite	horse	meat	donkey
corn	cherry	lion	potatoes	train	doll

Animals

Toys

Foods

Animals
1. _____
2. _____
3. _____
4. _____
5. _____
6. _____

Toys
1. _____
2. _____
3. _____
4. _____
5. _____
6. _____

Foods
1. _____
2. _____
3. _____
4. _____
5. _____
6. _____

Read the story and the summaries. Circle the best summary.

Matt loved to play in the water. Every time it rained, he would run outside to play in the puddles. He would splash water on his dog and the neighbor's cat. He would even splash water on anyone who came near. His friends would not play with him because he always got them wet. One day, a big truck went by and splashed water all over Matt. He got so wet he decided not to splash people anymore.

1. Matt liked to play in puddles of water. He got wet. He didn't splash anymore.

2. Matt liked to play in puddles of water. He splashed on animals and people. One day a truck splashed him. He stopped splashing others.

A thesaurus is a book that includes synonyms of words. You can use a thesaurus to make your writing more interesting. Look at this page from a thesaurus. Answer the questions below.

sad (adj): unhappy, down, dismal, morose, miserable, cheerless, gloomy, forlorn, dejected, glum, depressed

said (v): spoke, repeated, harped, yelled, whispered, echoed, bellowed, whined, shouted, told, sang, hammered, mentioned

1. Are the synonyms for the entry word in alphabetical order? _____

2. What does the **(adj)** after the word <u>sad</u> tell you about the word?_____

3. Rewrite this sentence using a synonym for the word <u>sad</u>:
   The boy was feeling sad because he lost his puppy.

   _____

Brooke saves buttons. Below are some she has collected. Read and solve the riddles. Write the letter of the button that matches the clues.

A   B   C   D   E   F

1. I do not have corners.
   I have 2 lines of symmetry.
   Which button am I ?___

2. I am not round.
   I have more than 4 corners.
   I show symmetry.
   Which button am I ?___

3. I have 4 corners.
   I have 2 lines of symmetry.
   Two sides are longer than
   the other 2 sides.
   Which button am I ?___

4. Now you write clues for
   the rest of the buttons. Can
   your friends and family
   guess?

Days of the week begin with capital letters. Fill in the blanks with the names of the days. Look at a calendar to help you spell them.

1. School days are _____, _____,
   _____, _____, and _____.

2. On what day of the week does
   Thanksgiving always fall? _____.

3. Write the names of the days that have six letters:
   _____, _____, and _____.

4. What day comes after Friday? _____.

5. Which days have eight letters? _____ and _____.

6. _____ has seven letters, and _____ has nine.

Word Referents. Read the sentences. Draw a circle around the word or words that the underlined word stands for.

EXAMPLE:

1. If you'll be home (Friday,) I'll see you <u>then</u>.

2. The fruit is really good; <u>it</u> tastes sweet.

3. Joe and Henry ran fast; <u>they</u> won the race.

4. When we found the park, Dad said, "Let's eat <u>here</u>."

5. Mary plays the piano; <u>she</u> plays very well.

6. I watered the flowers and put <u>them</u> on the bench.

7. Danny took the dog outside; he left the cat <u>there</u>, too.

8. The fish swam in the pond; <u>it</u> ate a bug.

Circle all the small words you can find in these words.

EXAMPLE:

(to)(wa)(r)(d)   (fo)(r)(est)

1. statement	2. infant	3. storage
4. spend	5. behind	6. million
7. bonnet	8. kittens	9. identify
10. penmanship	11. twinkled	12. balloon
13. friend	14. carpet	15. rabbit
16. spring	17. pinch	18. chocolate
19. kingdom	20. canyon	21. sentence

Subtract.

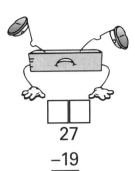 

EXAMPLE:

4|**11**	□□	□□	□□	□□	□□
5̶1̶	75	82	27	70	41
−38	−26	−37	−19	−24	−16
13					

□□	□□	□□	□□	□□	□□
65	83	95	56	22	38
− 9	−24	−78	−17	− 8	−19

□□	□□	□□	□□	□□	□□
81	54	64	35	87	60
− 6	−39	−18	−16	−48	−36

**Look at the geometric solids. Each side is called a face.
Write the number of faces each solid has.**

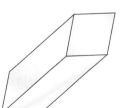

1. cube

_____ □ faces

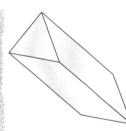

2. triangular prism

_____ △ faces _____ □ faces

3. rectangular prism

_____ □ faces _____ □ faces

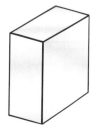

4. rectangular prism

_____ □ faces _____ □ faces

FACTOID
Crocodiles can't move their tongues.

Read each sentence and mark the correct one. Pay close attention to the commas.

1. Denise wanted five things in her lunch.
   _____ Denise got an apple, cake, an orange, carrots, and candy for her lunch.
   _____ Denise got an applecake, an orange, carrots, and candy for her lunch.

2. Grayson saw three children at the park.
   _____ Alex Lee, Henry, and John were playing ball.
   _____ Alex, Lee, Henry, and John were playing at the park.

3. Lori has four things in her room.
   _____ She has a basketball, a teddy bear, and a book.
   _____ She has a basket, a ball, a teddy bear, and a book.

Write these summer words in the boxes. Make sure they fit.

swimming
fishing
baseball
football
camping
vacation

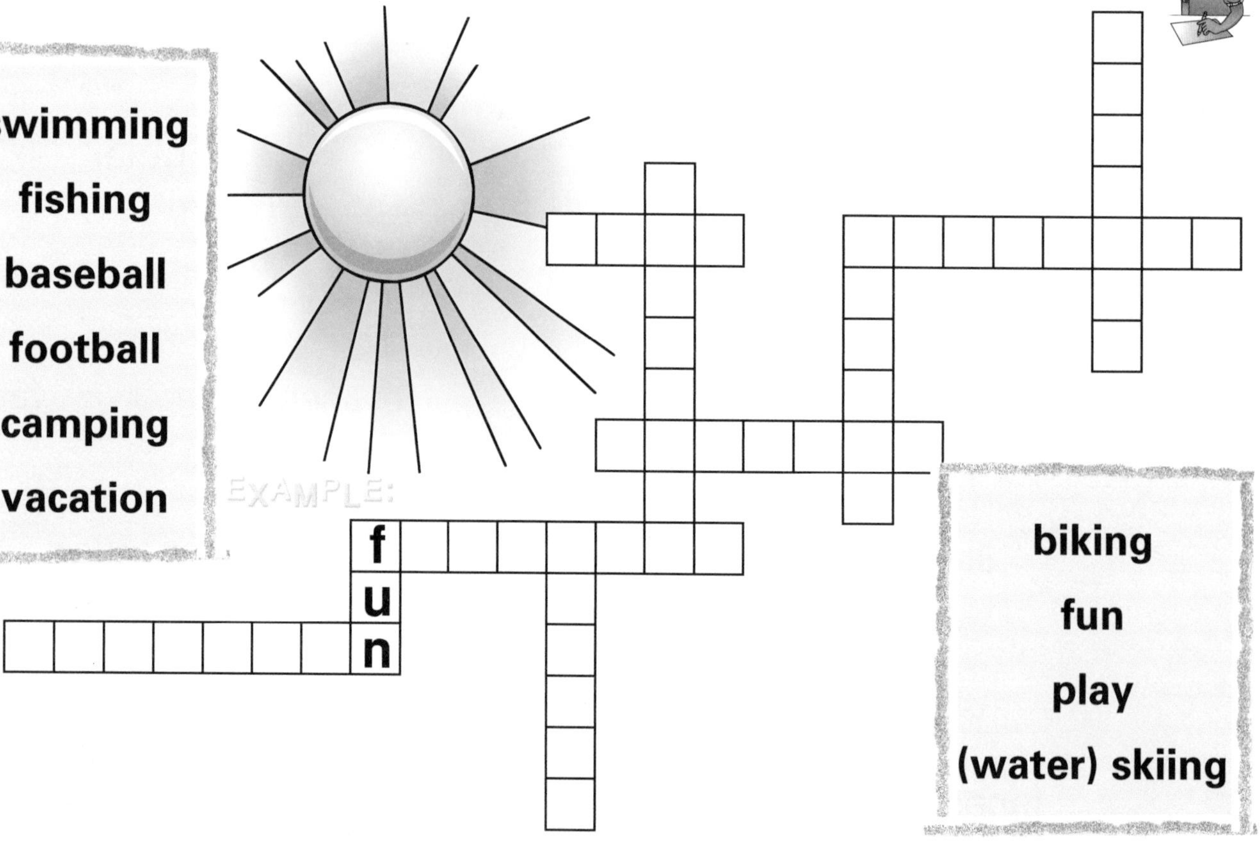

EXAMPLE:
f
u
n

biking
fun
play
(water) skiing

Count the money. Write in the amount for each line.

1.  _____ ¢

2.  _____ ¢

3.  _____ ¢

4.  _____ ¢

5.  _____ ¢

Change the order of each telling sentence to form a question. Remember the question mark.

EXAMPLE: The busy mailman is leaving. → Is the busy mailman leaving?

1. The old man is Gary's grandfather.

_____

2. Apples are red, round, and juicy.

_____

3. She can ride her shiny, new bike.

_____

4. I am going to ride a black horse.

_____

Fill in the blank with the correct word to complete each sentence.

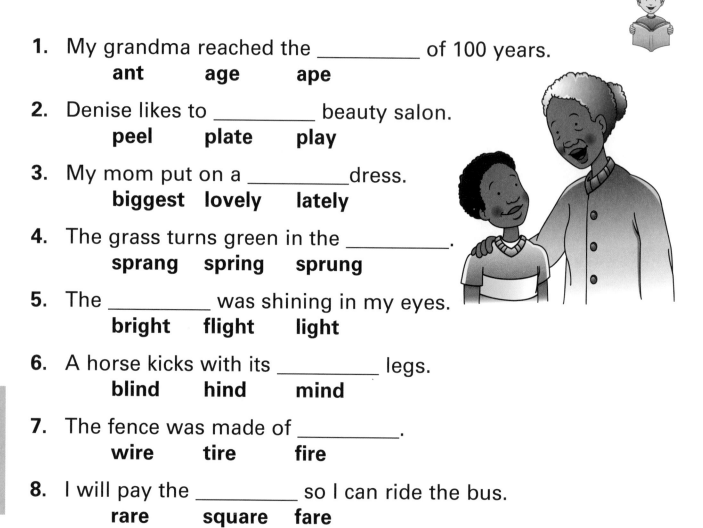

1. My grandma reached the _____ of 100 years.

    ant   age   ape

2. Denise likes to _____ beauty salon.

    peel   plate   play

3. My mom put on a _____ dress.

    biggest   lovely   lately

4. The grass turns green in the _____.

    sprang   spring   sprung

5. The _____ was shining in my eyes.

    bright   flight   light

6. A horse kicks with its _____ legs.

    blind   hind   mind

7. The fence was made of _____.

    wire   tire   fire

8. I will pay the _____ so I can ride the bus.

    rare   square   fare

Follow the directions to make a picture.

3.   .C

1. Draw a line from 3 to 5.
2. Draw a line from 3 to C to 9.
3. Draw a line from 3 to D.
4. Draw a line from D to Z to 5.
5. Draw a line from Z to 9.
6. Draw a line from 3 to R to D.
7. Draw a line from 3 to Z.
8. Color and add things you would take camping.

R.   5.

D.   Z.

Draw two straight lines to divide the square so each area totals...

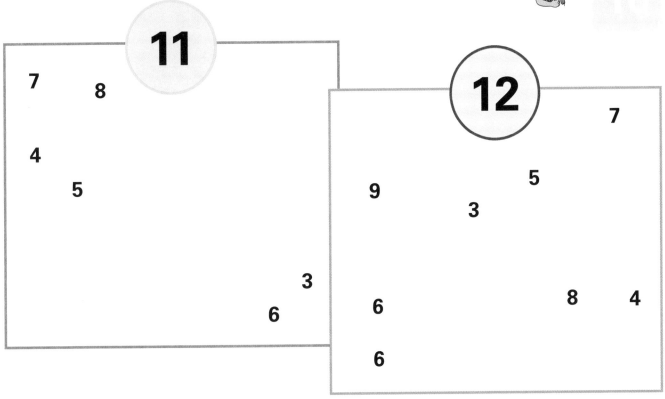

11

7   8

4

5

3

6

12

7

5

9

3

6

8   4

6

Abbreviations. To abbreviate a word means to shorten it. Match these abbreviations and words.

EXAMPLE:

December	Dr.	Mister	United States of America
Doctor	oz.	October	foot
Thursday	Dec.	ft.	Mr.
ounce	Jan.	Ave.	Avenue
January	Thur.	U.S.A.	Oct.

yd.	Junior	Saturday	Sr.
March	Wed.	Senior	St.
Jr.	yard	Monday	Mon.
inch	in.	Captain	Capt.
Wednesday	Mar.	street	Sat.

Read the sentences. Put a (.), (?), or (!) at the end of each sentence.

1. It will soon be the first day of school_____
2. Will Judy ride her bike to school this year_____
3. Have you had a fun summer vacation_____
4. My family went on a camping trip to the beach_____
5. Ann's sister will be starting school this year_____
6. What day will school start for you_____
7. Do you know the name of your new teacher_____
8. She will learn to be a teacher_____
9. Have you gone anywhere before_____
10. Have fun_____

Look at the parts of the bird, and then write them in alphabetical order.

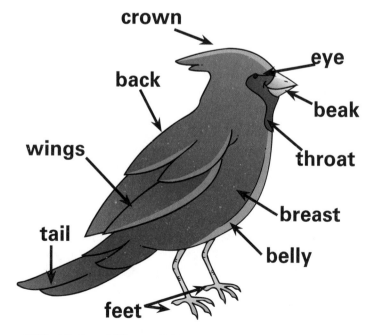

crown
back
wings
tail
feet
eye
beak
throat
breast
belly

1. _____
2. _____
3. _____
4. _____
5. _____
6. _____
7. _____
8. _____
9. _____
10. _____

Add or subtract. Be sure to start with the ones column.

33	62	19	53	67	58
+18	−28	+20	− 5	−38	+24

	44	34	72	75	47	81
	−18	− 9	+ 9	−47	−14	+11

31	28	46	31	54	7
−21	+14	− 6	−16	+27	+33

Use the correct word in each sentence. Some words need the helper has, have, or had.

was	is	Did	saw	gave
were	are	done	seen	given

1. I _____ my cousin Jamie.
2. Where _____ you going?
3. I have _____ many bugs crawling.
4. _____ you find your green pencil?
5. The one I lost _____ green.
6. That _____ the one I want.
7. He _____ me his new bike.
8. We have _____ all the candy away.
9. You _____ great, just great!
10. He has _____ it once again.

has

have

had

Change the spelling of the underlined words to make them plural.

mice
elves
leaves
knives
feet
teeth
geese
~~men~~

EXAMPLE:

1. one <u>man</u> or two   **men**

2. one <u>tooth</u> or three _____

3. one <u>leaf</u> or four _____

4. one <u>goose</u> or five _____

5. one <u>knife</u> or two _____

6. one <u>mouse</u> or six _____

7. one <u>elf</u> or four _____

8. one <u>foot</u> or nine _____

Pretend you live in a tree house! Write a story describing what it's like to live in your tree house:

_____

- -

_____

_____

_____

- -

_____

_____

_____

- -

_____

_____

_____

Place Value. Circle the number if:

7 is in the ones place

34 (177) (67) 76

84 (27) 42 (7) 16

6 is in the hundreds place

629	426	601	47
926	682	62	26
636	426	600	660

5 is in the tens place

126	54	151	555
38	185	250	58
859	50	725	255

9 is in the ones place

79	429	924	609
191	509	313	94
889	69	74	209

4 is in the hundreds place

1,423	484	124
2,642	1,600	432
3,046	4,422	144

3 is in the tens place

231	722	38	29
1,639	63	530	3
333	32	23	16

0 is in the tens place

50	101	609
1,406	10	804
36	420	99

7 is in the ones place

27	147	607
38	78	447
99	997	1,007

1 is in the tens place

1	211	184	1,121
71	17	130	6,191
140	100	501	122

Complete each sentence using <u>more than</u>, <u>less than</u>, or <u>equal to</u>. Write you answer on the line.

> **2 cups = 1 pint**
> **2 pints = 1 quart**
> **4 quarts = 1 gallon**

1. 2 pints are **equal to** 1 quart.

2. 1 pint is _____ 1 quart.

3. 3 quarts are _____ 1 gallon.

4. 3 cups are _____ 1 quart.

5. 1 gallon is _____ 1 pint.

6. 6 pints are _____ 3 quarts.

7. 2 pints are _____ 4 cups.

8. 8 quarts are _____ 2 gallons.

Read the words in the Word Box. Then write three telling sentences and three question sentences. Use a word from the Word Box in each of your sentences.

Word Box

silence
attention
calmly
famous
honor
strange
moment
station
million
free
sniffed
shiver

1. _____

_____

2. _____

_____

3. _____

_____

4. _____

_____

5. _____

_____

6. _____

_____

Describing Words. Words that describe tell something about other words in a sentence. Some words describe how things <u>look</u>. Some words describe how things <u>sound</u>. Some words describe how things feel or how things <u>taste</u>. Circle the describing words in these sentences.

1. The shrill whistle hurt my ears.

2. That sad child must be lost.

3. Joe likes a soft pillow.

4. Our class climbed a steep hill.

5. The door made a screechy noise.

6. That fluffy yellow kitten is mine.

7. The hot, wet sand felt good on our feet.

8. The sour lemon made my mouth water.

EXAMPLE:
The (big)(red) wagon rolled down the hill.

(<u>Big</u> and <u>red</u> tell how the wagon looks.)

Use an inch ruler. Measure the lines between the dots. Round to the nearest inch. Write the measurements in the boxes and add them together.

☐ + ☐ + ☐ = _____ inches

☐ + ☐ + ☐ = _____ inches

☐ + ☐ + ☐ = _____ inches

Sometimes Y is a vowel. Can you circle the word that is spelled correctly in each row?

EXAMPLE:

1. (sunny)	suny	sunnie
2. pretty	pritty	prety
3. kary	cary	carry
4. sily	silly	selly
5. whi	why	whhy
6. try	trie	trhi
7. bodie	body	boddy
8. funy	funnie	funny
9. crie	cri	cry

Who is talking in the following sentences? Write the name on the line. The first one is done for you.

1. Grayson said, "Tanner, you need to go to bed." __**Grayson**__

2. "Is this your book, Allie?" asked Denise. _____

3. Allie replied, "No, Denise, it is not my book." _____

4. The dog barked, "This is my house, cat, go away!" _____

5. "Would you please go to the store for me?" Mother asked. _____

6. "Denise," said Father, "Mr. Fredrickson wants us to go to the zoo with him. Lori, would you like to go, too?" _____

7. "I want to eat now," I said. "I can't wait." _____

8. "Is it hard to ride a bike, Grandpa?" asked Matt. _____

9. "No," said Grandpa. "Not if you practice a lot." _____

Use a ruler to connect the dots between matching numbers and letters. See what design you make. Color it if you like.

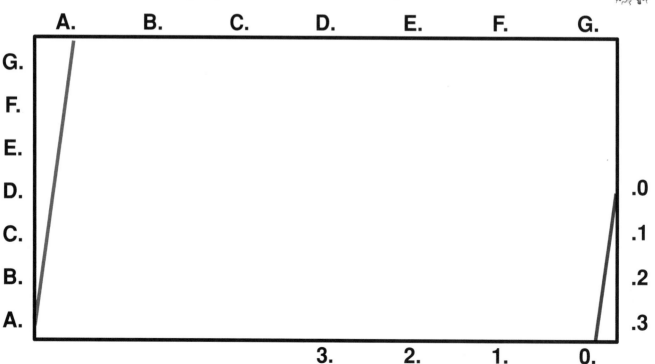

Write the time or draw the hands.

9:25   _____ : _____   **6:35**

 one hour later →   one hour later →

4:50   _____ : _____   **11:10**   _____ : _____

Homophones are words that sound the same, but are spelled differently. Fill in each blank with the homophone of the underlined word. Use the words from the box.

EXAMPLE:

1. Did you <u>write</u> down the _____**right**_____ answer?

2. I can<u>not</u> tie a _____ with this rope.

3. Don only <u>won</u> _____ game.

4. <u>Would</u> you cut some _____ for the stove?

5. <u>Be</u> careful, or that _____ will sting you!

6. I <u>knew</u> I would get some _____ shoes.

7. Our <u>maid</u> has already _____ my bed.

8. We saw a man fight a <u>bear</u> with his _____ hands.

bee	wood	bare	knot
~~right~~	one	new	made

Add -less or -ness to the base word in the sentence (-less and -ness are common suffixes).

EXAMPLE:

1. I took the ___home**less**___ kitten to my house.

2. The children were very ___rest___ today.

3. The ___friendli___ of the people made us feel at home.

4. Trying to train my dog to sit up is ___hope___.

5. The baby loves the ___soft___ of her blanket.

6. The ___loud___ of the noise made me jump.

7. Her ___happi___ showed on her face.

8. My ___forgetful___ is going to get me in trouble.

Draw the other half of the picture to match.

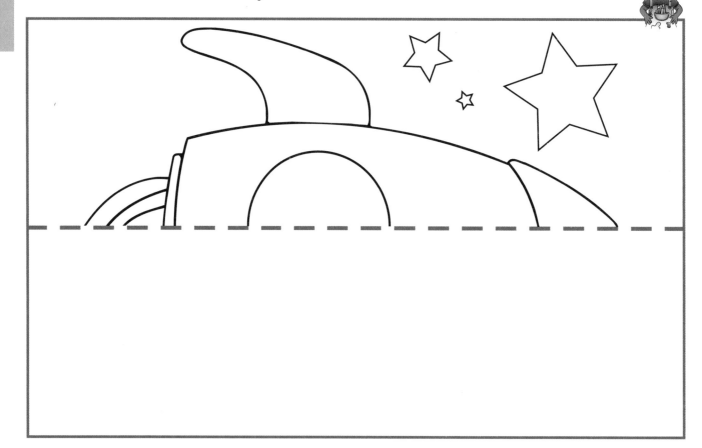

Disappearing Act

You may know that water can disappear by evaporating. Do you know that sometimes it leaves stuff behind when it disappears?

Stuff You Need:

drinking glass
masking tape
pencil
2 pie tins
salt
spoon
tablespoon
water

Here's What to Do:

1. Use the masking tape and a pencil to label the outside bottom of two pie tins. Label pie tin #1 "saltwater" and pie tin #2 "tap water."

2. Add enough water to pie tin #2 to just cover the bottom. Then set it aside. Record the amount of water that you use, and use the same amount for pie tin #1.

3. For pie tin #1, pour warm water into a drinking glass. Add a tablespoon of salt to the water. Stir it until it is completely dissolved. Keep adding salt until no more will dissolve. This is called a saturated solution. Pour your saturated solution into pie tin #1.

4. Set both pie tins aside. Record your observations every day until all of the liquid in both pie tins has completely evaporated.

What's This All About?

This activity uses saltwater as the basis for crystal formation. The water evaporates from the pan, and the mineral, salt, is left.

More Fun Ideas to Try:

1. Change the amount of salt in the saltwater. See if it affects the rate of evaporation. Be sure to use the same amount of water each time; just change the amount of salt used.

2. You can also vary the liquid you use. Try vinegar, ammonia, etc. When you do this, make sure that you use the same amount of salt and only change the liquid.

Eggshell Geodes

Geodes are rocks with beautiful crystal formations inside. Would you like to see how a geode is made?

Stuff You Need:

adult
copper sulfate crystals (1 lb.)
egg carton
eggshell halves
hot pad (oven mitt)
metal food can (like a coffee can)
spoon
stove top
water

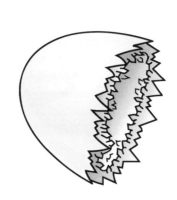

Here's What to Do:

1. Add 2 pints of water to your metal food can. Place it on the stove top.

Don't forget to use caution when using the stove! Make sure an adult is nearby!

2. Let the water boil; then slowly add the copper sulfate crystals. Stir the solution constantly. As the crystals dissolve, add more. Add copper sulfate until the crystals won't dissolve anymore.

3. Get clean eggshell halves and put them in the egg carton for support. Pour the copper sulfate solution up to the top of each eggshell.

4. Carefully set them aside. Watch the solution evaporate. When all the solution has evaporated, you will have something that resembles a geode.

What's This All About?

A geode is a mineral deposit that is formed when a gas bubble is trapped in a lava flow. Over time, the bubble fills with mineral water and evaporates, again and again. Each time this happens, crystals begin to form.

Motivational Calendar

Month

My parents and I decided that if I complete
15 days of **Summer Bridge Activities**™ and
read _____ minutes a day, my incentive/reward will be:

Child's Signature _____   Parent's Signature_____

Day 1	☆	📖	_____	Day 9	☆	📖	_____
Day 2	☆	📖	_____	Day 10	☆	📖	_____
Day 3	☆	📖	_____	Day 11	☆	📖	_____
Day 4	☆	📖	_____	Day 12	☆	📖	_____
Day 5	☆	📖	_____	Day 13	☆	📖	_____
Day 6	☆	📖	_____	Day 14	☆	📖	_____
Day 7	☆	📖	_____	Day 15	☆	📖	_____
Day 8	☆	📖	_____				

Child: Color the ☆ for daily activities completed.
Color the 📖 for daily reading completed.

Parent: Initial the ____ when all activities are complete.

Discover Something New!

Fun Activity Ideas to Go Along with the Third Section!

 1 Write a thank-you note to last year's teacher.

 2 Make homemade root beer.

 3 Visit the library. Research an occupation.

 4 Visit someone in your chosen occupation.

 5 Have a neighborhood barbecue.

6 Contact your city hall and do some volunteer work.

7 Try a midweek campout.

8 Go to a farm and feed the animals.

9 Plan a neighborhood bicycle olympics.

10 Share your garden produce with your neighbors.

 11 Remember your times tables. Practice.

 12 Have a marble tournament.

 13 Make and fly a paper airplane.

 14 Visit a fish hatchery.

 15 Have a backyard breakfast.

Write the signs for greater than (>), less than (<), or equal to (=) in the circles.

EXAMPLE:

7 + 7 (<) 15   9 + 7 ◯ 16   8 + 9 ◯ 18

8 + 6 (=) 14   13 − 4 ◯ 10   10 − 4 ◯ 6

15 (>) 1 + 9   16 + 4 ◯ 17   17 − 9 ◯ 8

8 + 9 ◯ 9 + 8   5 + 8 ◯ 6 + 7   15 − 5 ◯ 13 − 4

11 − 4 ◯ 6 + 2   12 − 6 ◯ 6 + 6   18 − 8 ◯ 8 + 8

12 − 1 ◯ 12 − 6   10 + 1 ◯ 4 + 7   9 + 3 ◯ 14 − 7

Read the story. Complete the picture to go with the story.

Mary planted flowers in each pot. They grew fast. She put the flowers all in a row. The white flower was in the middle. The purple flower was second. The orange flower was not first. The yellow flower was last. Where was the pink flower? Where does the orange flower go?

Doing words are called <u>verbs</u>. Some doing words mean to do it now or later; others mean we already did it. Put each doing word on the correct ladder.

FACTOID
Snail slime is so thick because it protects the snail's soft "foot."

EXAMPLE:

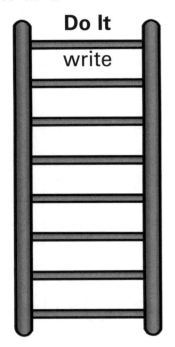

Do It

write

laughed   wore

~~write~~   know

knew   flew

blew   found

wear   blow

~~wrote~~   find

fly   laugh

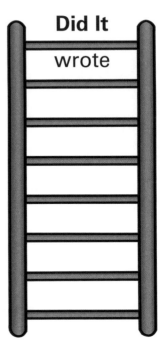

Did It

wrote

Add <u>-ed</u>, or <u>-ing</u> to the following base words. Be careful. Words that end in <u>-n</u>, <u>-g</u>, and <u>-p</u> may need an additional letter. Those ending in <u>-e</u> may change also.

EXAMPLE:

rake	jump	hug	cook	skate
raked				
raking				

wrap	sneeze	pop	walk	smile

Use a centimeter ruler. Find the length of each object.

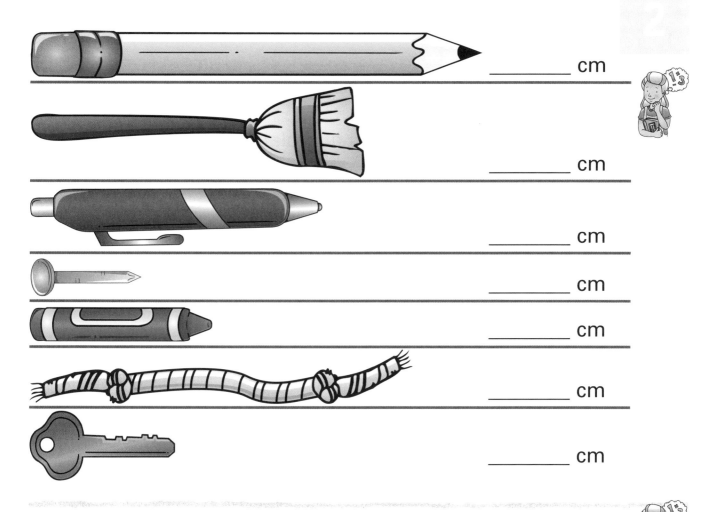

_____ cm

_____ cm

_____ cm

_____ cm

_____ cm

_____ cm

_____ cm

<u>Cardinal</u> <u>numbers</u> tell us how many or how much we have of something. They can be written in number (80) or word form (eighty). <u>Ordinal</u> <u>numbers</u> tell us "which one" a number is in a series. For example, if I have five apples in a row, the number three apple is the <u>third</u> apple in the row. (<u>Third</u> is an ordinal number.)

Write the number, number word, or ordinal number in the blank.

1. _____ _____ seventieth

2. 45 _____ _____

3. _____ thirty-six _____

Write these sentences correctly. Don't forget the capital letters, periods, question marks, commas, and quotation marks.

1. randy has five pets: a dog cat rabbit and two mice

2. do bluebirds eat seeds insects and plants

3. would you please go to the store for me asked grayson

4. my name is allie and I like candy

Write the following words under the correct heading:	(opposite) Antonyms	(sound alike) Homophones	(mean the same) Synonyms
EXAMPLE: would wood		would wood	
1. high low			
2. pile heap			
3. weight wait			
4. blend mix			
5. empty full			
6. difficult hard			
7. rain reign			
8. cool warm			
9. crawl creep			
10. groan grown			

Color in the correct fraction for each picture.

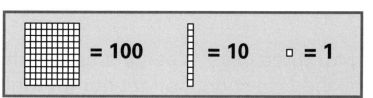

= 100   = 10   □ = 1

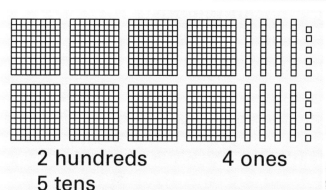

2 hundreds   4 ones
5 tens

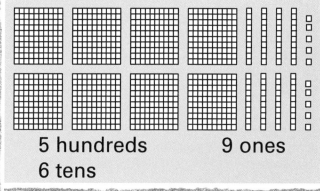

5 hundreds   9 ones
6 tens

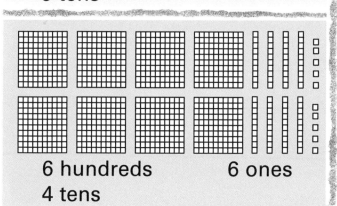

6 hundreds   6 ones
4 tens

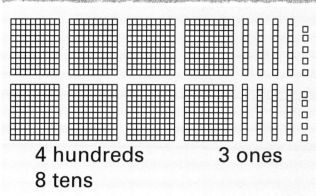

4 hundreds   3 ones
8 tens

Read each word. Look at the underlined letter or letters and change them to make a new word. Read them to your parents.

EXAMPLE:

take **bake**   press _____   well _____

prize _____   dove _____   quick _____

rise _____   cost _____   wish _____

those _____   shell _____   ship _____

true _____   bud _____   truck _____

Read the story. Then number the events in the order they happened.

It had snowed for three days. When it stopped, the snow was so deep Tom and Don could not get out through the door of the cabin. The men had to climb out the upstairs window in order to get outside. They spent hours shoveling the snow away from the cabin door. At last, they were able to get the door open.

( ) The men climbed out the window.

( ) It snowed for three days.

( ) Don and Tom got the door open.

( ) The men shoveled snow for hours.

Doors, Doors, Doors. There are many kinds of doors belonging to many interesting places and things: cars, houses, barns, bedrooms, and basements.

Think of a door that could "lead" you to an interesting place or a strange thing. Draw a picture of your door and what's behind it.

Subtract.

758	410	894	978	879	646
− 126	− 310	− 251	− 165	− 704	− 16
632	100	643	813	175	630

785	583	957	683	896	923
− 223	− 161	− 140	− 611	− 840	− 111
562	422	817	072	56	812

686	349	867	539	767	297
− 255	− 104	− 36	− 39	− 10	− 177
431	245	831	500	757	120

Words That Go Together. Write the correct word.

EXAMPLE:

1. <u>Car</u> is to <u>road</u> as <u>boat</u> is to _____**lake**_____.

2. <u>Cloud</u> is to <u>sky</u> as <u>worm</u> is to _____.

3. <u>City</u> is to <u>buildings</u> as <u>forest</u> is to _____.

4. <u>Knob</u> is to <u>door</u> as <u>pane</u> is to _____.

5. <u>Cub</u> is to <u>bear</u> as <u>calf</u> is to _____.

6. <u>Bus</u> is to <u>car</u> as <u>airplane</u> is to _____.

7. <u>Quack</u> is to <u>duck</u> as <u>meow</u> is to _____.

8. <u>Squirrel</u> is to <u>nut</u> as <u>cow</u> is to _____.

Word Bank

cat

ground

hay

window

~~lake~~

trees

cow

jet

Finish writing the correct word in each sentence by changing the last letter and adding the correct ending.

Word List

drier

happiest

easier

tried

carried

flies

worries

funniest

1. Wanda showed me the __funn~~x~~iest__ picture.

2. My clothes are __dry__ than yours.

3. That bird __fly__ south for the winter.

4. Joe __worry__ about his sick friend.

5. My book is __easy__ to read than yours.

6. This was my __happy__ birthday ever!

7. Pete __carry__ his books to school.

8. I __try__ to get the door unstuck.

Find the -ack, -ick, -ock, -uck, and -eck words in the search puzzle. Circle them. Then fill in the blanks with words from the word box.

w	b	a	c	k	z	y	r
r	s	t	u	c	k	w	o
e	k	o	k	o	m	i	c
c	c	r	b	s	q	c	k
k	i	s	p	e	c	k	d
l	l	u	c	k	c	c	u
p	e	c	k	a	x	w	c
y	l	u	p	c	h	d	k

rock	duck	peck
wick	back	luck
lick	pack	sock
stuck	speck	wreck

The _____

put her _____

on the _____.

Add.

324	973	777	206	88	548
+125	+ 24	+112	+132	+171	+241
449	997	889	338	259	789

420	623	621	230	175	422
+337	+125	+126	+362	+113	+561
757	748	747	592	258	983

803	603	9	300	540	921
+104	+292	+600	+500	+ 7	+157
907	895	609	800	547	1078

Is the underlined word spelled right or wrong? Mark your answer. Correct the words that are wrong by writing them correctly in the space provided.

		right	wrong
EXAMPLE:			
1. Marcus has a new <u>electrik</u> car.	electric	○	●
2. Sara takes the fast <u>trane</u> to work.	_____	○	○
3. Don't <u>break</u> the glass, please.	_____	○	○
4. The cat was <u>thein</u> because it didn't eat.	_____	○	○
5. Let's all <u>keap</u> together when we go.	_____	○	○
6. I want my hair to grow very <u>long</u>.	_____	○	○
7. I hit the fence with my <u>stick</u>.	_____	○	○
8. My dad has a large dump <u>truke</u>.	_____	○	○
9. You don't <u>beleve</u> I can run fast.	_____	○	○
10. Let's run and <u>plae</u>.	_____	○	○

Read the story and fill in the blanks using the word list below.

cockatoos	zoo	you	spray	copy	jump
monkeys	colorful	lions	zoo	down	

When you go to the _____, you watch the animals, and they watch you. The elephants may _____ you with water. The _____ swing by their tails. They try to do what you do. Scratch your head, and they will _____ you and do it, too. Jump up and _____, and they will _____, too. My favorite animals at the zoo are the _____. My favorite birds are the _____. They are bright and _____. I love to go to the _____! Don't _____?

Write titles for the following lists.

EXAMPLE:

Birds

robin	needle	soap	milk
wren	thread	water	soda
blue jay	scissors	washcloth	water
canary	thimble	towel	juice

whale	lions	ice	mother
shark	tigers	snow	father
dolphin	bears	frost	sister
minnow	elephants	snowman	brother

One meter is 100 centimeters. Circle what you think.

EXAMPLE:

Is a real tree—

(taller than one meter)

or shorter than one meter?

1. Are you—

   taller than one meter

   or shorter than one meter?

2. Is a real puppy—

   longer than one meter

   or shorter than one meter?

3. Is your bedroom door—

   taller than one meter

   or shorter than one meter?

4. Is the pencil or pen you are using—

   longer than one meter

   or shorter than one meter?

5. Is this line—

   longer than one meter

   or shorter than one meter?

Write the two words that make up the contractions.

1. hasn't _____

2. I'm _____

3. you'll _____

4. wouldn't _____

5. we've _____

6. let's _____

7. you're _____

8. she's _____

9. isn't _____

10. won't _____

11. doesn't _____

12. you've _____

Put the words in alphabetical order so the sentences make sense. Write the sentences. Be sure to put a capital letter on the first word.

EXAMPLE:

1. talk did she with you? _____ **Did she talk with you?** _____

2. I notebook there left my. _____

3. babies walkers cute in are? _____

4. wildflowers the Allie smelled. _____

5. turtles sneaky I love. _____

6. player zip runs baseball a with. _____

   _____

7. drink do milk dragons? _____

8. water careful in be the. _____

It's your birthday. Blow out your candles and make a wish! Write about your wish and/or draw a picture of it.

Hundreds, Tens, and Ones.

EXAMPLE: Circle the numbers that are in the tens place. 5③6 ⑧4 1,6⓪2	1. Circle the numbers that are in the ones place. 26 842 163 924 19 846
2. Circle the numbers that are in the hundreds place. 481 643 970 1294 1,122	3. Circle the numbers that are in the tens place. 816 121 6,211 44 729 4,864
4. What does the circled number mean? 51⑥ 6 ones 6 hundreds 6 tens	5. What does the circled number mean? ②65 2 ones 2 tens 2 hundreds
6. What does the circled number mean? 2⓪1 0 ones 0 hundreds 0 tens	7. **707** _____ tens _____ hundreds _____ ones
EXAMPLE: Tell how many. 100 100 10 10 1 **221**	8. **846** _____ tens _____ hundreds _____ ones
9. Tell how many. 100 100 10 10 1 1 _____	10. **301** _____ tens _____ hundreds _____ ones

Probability. Look at the spinner. Answer the questions.

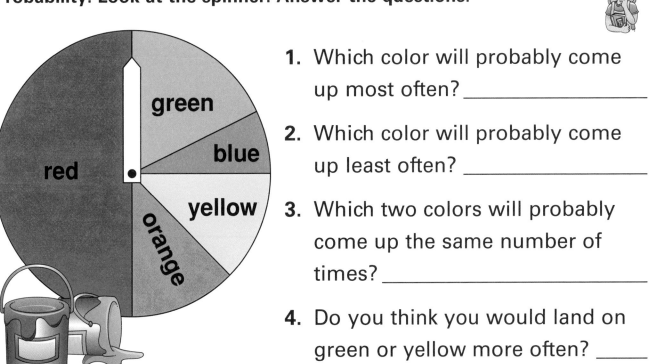

1. Which color will probably come up most often? _____

2. Which color will probably come up least often? _____

3. Which two colors will probably come up the same number of times? _____

4. Do you think you would land on green or yellow more often? _____

Read the story and answer the questions.

  Lori got up late today, so she missed the bus. She had to walk to school. She was tired and cranky when she got there. She promised herself that she would never sleep late again.

1. Why did Lori miss the bus?

_____

- -

_____

2. Why did she have to walk?

_____

- -

_____

3. What advice do you have for Lori?

_____

- -

_____

Let's make a sandwich. Number the sentences in the correct order. The first one has been done for you.

_____ Put whatever else you like on your sandwich.

__1__ Take two pieces of bread. Put butter on top of each.

_____ Put the two pieces of bread together.

_____ Next put on the meat and cheese.

_____ Eat your sandwich—yum, yum!

_____ Cut the sandwich in two and put it on a plate.

_____ Clean up after yourself.

Write the signs for greater than (>), less than (<), or equal to (=) in the circles.

EXAMPLE:

386 ⊘ 367	474 ◯ 447	184 ◯ 284
254 ◯ 245	442 ◯ 542	898 ◯ 889
780 ◯ 870	501 ◯ 710	999 ◯ 1,000

 ◯  ◯  ◯

9 tens ◯ 10 fives	3 fives ◯ 2 tens	25 ones ◯ 4 tens
10 tens ◯ 8 fives	4 tens ◯ 18 ones	8 tens ◯ 12 fives
14 fives ◯ 10 tens	1 hundred ◯ 6 tens	3 hundreds ◯ 20 tens

Read the words. Write down how many vowels you see and then how many vowel sounds you hear.

	vowels	vowel sounds		vowels	vowel sounds
puzzle	_____	_____	radio	_____	_____
possible	_____	_____	candy	_____	_____
cookies	_____	_____	sneeze	_____	_____
alphabet	_____	_____	wanted	_____	_____
games	_____	_____	heart	_____	_____
jump	_____	_____	useful	_____	_____
pilot	_____	_____	beautiful	_____	_____

Antonyms are opposites. Read the sentences. Circle the word that will complete the sentence.

1. Be sure to (blame, praise) your friends when they do good work.

2. If you don't go now, I will not (allow, refuse) you to go again.

3. Mother told me to wear (dirty, clean) clothes to the party.

4. Troy knows how to take charge of the group. He is a very good (follower, leader).

5. When the light is red, you must remember to (go, stop).

6. The library is a place where we need to be (noisy, quiet).

7. The bread was so old, it became (fresh, stale).

8. While I'm gone, would you please (answer, question) the phone?

Following Directions.

toucan   **puffin**   **kingfisher**

1. Color the kingfisher's head and wings blue green. Color his breast red orange. Leave his throat white. Color his bill yellow orange. Draw a post for him to stand on.

2. Color the toucan's bill any three colors you wish. Color his throat and breast orange. Color around his eye green. Color the rest of him black, except for his feet. Draw a branch for him to sit on.

3. Color the puffin's bill green, red, and yellow. Leave his head, breast, and feet white. Color the rest of him black, but not too dark. Draw some ice under the puffin's feet.

4. Color all the birds' feet orange.

Add or subtract.

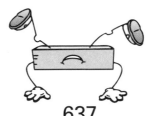

573	832	153	637	638	721
−132	+ 23	+210	−224	−532	+112
441	855	363	413	106	833

35	263	508	337	544	206
− 25	+ 13	−305	+231	−234	+392
10	276	203	568	310	598

972	684	912	400	805	978
−421	−182	+ 87	+500	−202	−326
551	502	999	900	603	652

Find the hidden sentences and write them on the lines.
Remember capital letters and periods.

1.

I	C
L	A
I	N
K	D
E	Y

2.

D	A	N	I
U	R	N	M
C	E	Y	A
K	F	A	L
S	U	N	S

3.

P	N	H	I	A	M	S	O
L	G	M	E	N	I	A	F
A	W	Y	N	D	L	L	F
Y	I	F	D	F	Y	O	U
I	T	R	S	A	I	T	N

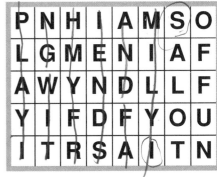

1. ___I like candy.___

2. ___Ducks are funny animals.___

3. ___Playing with my friends and family___
___is___

Read the sentences and decide whether they are real or make-believe.

BRICKS

1. Bricks come in different colors. Some are red, yellow, gray, or white. People used to have only red brick houses. Now people use other colors, too.

☐ **real** ☐ **make-believe**

3. People can make walls and fences out of bricks. Brick walls and fences are very strong. They seldom break or crumble.

☐ **real** ☐ **make-believe**

2. The oldest little pig made his house of bricks to keep out the big, bad wolf. He locked the door and was safe. He lived happily ever after.

☐ **real** ☐ **make-believe**

Grid Artwork. Try to copy the picture.

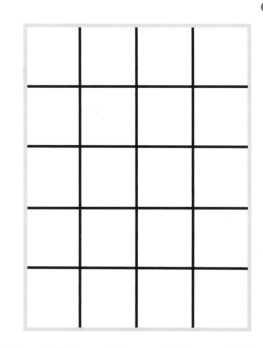

Match and multiply.

EXAMPLE:

4 x 3 = _____

3 x 3 = _____

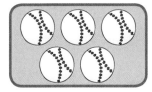 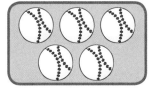 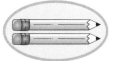

5 x 2 = _____

3 x 2 = _____

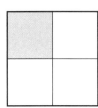  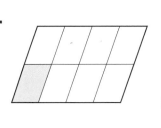

2 x 5 = _____

Circle or write the name of the fraction that names or shows the shaded part of each whole shape.

1. $\frac{1}{2}$

$\left(\frac{1}{4}\right)$

$\frac{1}{10}$

2. $\frac{1}{2}$

$\frac{1}{4}$

$\left(\frac{1}{3}\right)$

3. 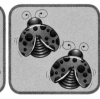 $\frac{1}{10}$

$\frac{1}{3}$

$\left(\frac{1}{8}\right)$

4.  $\frac{1}{2}$

5. 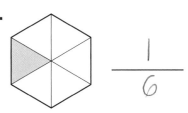 $\frac{1}{6}$

6. 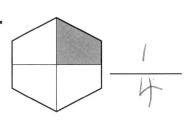 $\frac{1}{4}$

Mark the vowels: —short, —long, or /silent. The first two are done for you.

FACTOID
Every 2,000 pounds of recycled paper saves about 16 trees.

1. hōlé

2. cŭt

3. railroad

4. tube

5. music

6. mop

7. meat

8. fly

9. think

10. use

11. catch

12. clock

13. children

14. these

15. smile

16. gave

17. find

18. glad

19. which

20. leave

21. much

Write down all of the sound words in Matt's story.

Matt heard the wind howling outside and the ringing of the telephone inside. He heard his mother and father talking softly. His sister was singing to their baby brother, who was crying in his crib. The fish in the fish tank were gurgling to one another as the dog barked for something to eat. Matt decided you could hear a lot of interesting things if you just listen.

_____

_____

_____

_____

_____

_____

Color the items in each box to match the fraction.

EXAMPLE:

Color one-third.

$\frac{1}{3}$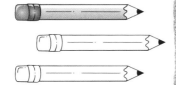

Color two-fourths.

$\frac{2}{4}$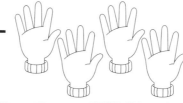

Color three-sixths.

$\frac{3}{6}$

Color seven-tenths.

$\frac{7}{10}$

Color one-fourth.

$\frac{1}{4}$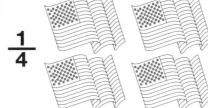

Color five-eighths.

$\frac{5}{8}$

Color three-sevenths.

$\frac{3}{7}$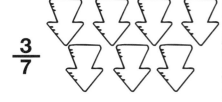

Color one-half.

$\frac{1}{2}$

Color two-thirds.

$\frac{2}{3}$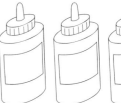

Read the following sentences and use the _qu-_ words to fill in the blanks.

1. The little pigs like to _____.

2. _____ the oranges to make juice.

3. I have a colorful _____ on my bed.

4. Sh, be very _____.

5. Two dimes and a nickel make a _____.

6. The king and _____ sit on thrones.

7. The door has a _____.

8. A _____ has four corners.

9. I would like to ask a _____.

10. Tests are a type of _____.

question
queen
quiet
quarter
squeal
squeak
square
quiz
quilt
squeeze

Finish the "I could..." sentences.

FACTOID
Hair is one of the fastest-growing tissues in the body.

1. I could fish if I had a _____ .

2. I could write if I had a _____ .

3. I could play if I had a _____ .

4. I could swim if I had a _____ .

5. I could jump if I had a _____ .

6. I could eat if I had a _____ .

7. I could read if I had a _____ .

8. I could color if I had a _____ .

Draw lines to connect syllables and make complete words.

1.	pen	met	2.	car	en	3.	can	cus
	sun	cil		pup	rot		sis	fin
	hel	gon		can	py		muf	dle
	dra	dae		sev	dy		cir	ter

3.	blos	som	4.	won	ry	6.	pea	dow
	rab	der		sum	der		dol	lar
	spi	bit		crick	mer		mit	ten
	fun	ny		mar	et		win	nuts

Pretend you are the teacher. With a red pencil correct this paper: _X_ wrong _C_ correct.

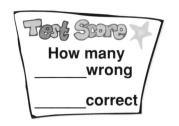

EXAMPLE:

```
   423        784        434        324         38        522
  +138       -107       +128       +267        +19       +139
   561 C      618 X      562        592         57        760
```

```
   667        410        948        546        634        315
  -419       -125       -819       -317       -571       -142
   247        305        129        218         63        173
```

```
   342        467        861        933        429        193
  -237       +161       -671       -673       +364       +184
   105        628        210        260        893        377
```

Draw a line to match each shape on the left to the shape on the right that shows the same fraction.

 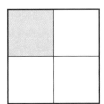 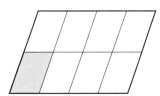 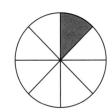

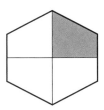 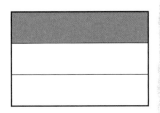 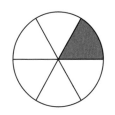 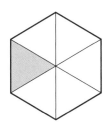

Read the following story and then underline the sentence that tells what the story is about.

All birds are alike in some ways and different in others. They all have wings, but not all of them fly. Some are tame, and some are wild. Some birds sing. Some talk. Some are gentle; others are not so gentle. Some fly very high and far; others do not. Some birds are colorful, while others are quite drab.

a. Some birds are tame; others are not.
b. All birds are strange and colorful.
c. Birds are alike and different from each other.

Which Meaning? Match the correct meaning with the correct sentence.

EXAMPLE:

fly	1. a small insect	__2__ The birds can <u>fly</u>.
	2. to move through the air	__1__ The spider ate the <u>fly</u>.
foot	1. a part of the body	___ This is a <u>foot</u>-long hot dog.
	2. 12 inches in measurement	___ My left <u>foot</u> hurts.
box	1. a container	___ Put the gift in this <u>box</u>.
	2. to hit with the fists	___ Don't <u>box</u>. You'll get hurt.
pitch	1. tar or sap	___ <u>Pitch</u> me the ball.
	2. to throw or toss	___ <u>Pitch</u> is on the tree.
store	1. a market	___ <u>Store</u> the books on a shelf.
	2. to put away for the future	___ I bought a dress at the <u>store</u>.
well	1. healthy, not sick	___ Drop a penny in the <u>well</u>.
	2. a hole to collect water	___ Are you feeling <u>well</u>?

Read and answer.

EXAMPLE: There are 3 cages with 2 rabbits in each cage. How many rabbits are there in all?

__3__ x __2__ = ☐ 6 ☐ rabbits

1. Allie has 3 vases with 4 flowers in each vase. How many flowers does she have in all?

____ x ____ = ☐ flowers

2. Denise has 4 packages of gum with 5 pieces in each package. How many pieces does she have?

____ x ____ = ☐ pieces

3. Dad has 3 glasses. He put 2 straws in each glass. How many straws did Dad put in the glasses?

____ x ____ = ☐ straws

4. Mother made 3 shirts. She put 3 buttons on each shirt. How many buttons did Mother use?

____ x ____ = ☐ buttons

5. We have 4 tables for the party. Each table needs 4 chairs. How many chairs do we need in all?

____ x ____ = ☐ chairs

Make a graph to tell about Farmer George's farm. Color one square for each animal in the picture.

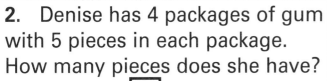

6						
5						
4						
3						
2						
1						
0						

Connect the sentence with the correct word from the box.

EXAMPLE:

1. This lets you talk to someone far away.
2. This is something you can walk through when you are home.
3. This is the opposite of <u>back</u>.
4. This is what you might do when you are sad.
5. This is something that is found all around you.
6. This is your mom or dad's sister.
7. When something itches, you usually do this.

Word List

scratch

cry

phone

front

door

air

aunt

Writing a sentence in which all the words start with the same letter can be fun. EXAMPLE: **Freddy farmer fixes flats.**

Try your skills with these letters:

1. **C**
   _____
   _____

2. **I**
   _____
   _____

3. **S**
   _____
   _____

4. **T**
   _____
   _____

5. **R**
   _____
   _____
   _____

Multiply.

1. 5 x 1 = _____   **2.** 5 x 5 = _____   **3.** 2 x 3 = _____

1 x 0 = _____   2 x 2 = _____   3 x 4 = _____

4 x 2 = _____   3 x 3 = _____   4 x 5 = _____

0 x 1 = _____   1 x 1 = _____   2 x 5 = _____

3 x 5 = _____   4 x 1 = _____   1 x 2 = _____

4.

3	4	3	6	7	2	5	4
x 5	x 5	x 4	x 2	x 1	x 3	x 5	x 0

5.   2 x 4 = ___   1 x 3 = ___   5 x 3 = ___

5 x 6 = ___   2 x 6 = ___   0 x 5 = ___

Recognizing Syllables. Record how many vowels, vowel sounds, and syllables are in each word. Remember: There are as many syllables in a word as there are vowel sounds.

△ = number of vowels   □ = number of syllables   ○ = number of vowels sounds

EXAMPLE:

goat   ② 1 ①   uncle   △ □ ○

potato △ □ ○   mailbox △ □ ○

raccoon △ □ ○   dentist △ □ ○

giant   △ □ ○   tree   △ □ ○

umbrella △ □ ○   racquetball △ □ ○

cupcake △ □ ○   sandbox △ □ ○

Read each sentence. Write the correct answer.

1. Sam's going to Paul's football game.

   Who is going to the game? _____

   Whose game is it? _____

2. Susan's taking care of Joyce's baby.

   To whom does the baby belong? _____

   Who's taking care of the baby? _____

3. She's singing the teacher's favorite song.

   Whose favorite song is she singing? _____

   Who is singing? _____

4. Al is reading Sam's books.

   Who do the books belong to? _____

   Who is reading? _____

Hot Summer Suns. Write a word or words on each sun that tell something you are doing or would like to do in the summer.

swimming
reading

Add or subtract.

462	483	746	762	821	563
+ 128	− 280	+ 222	+ 29	− 530	− 125

	236	924	233	407	852	365
	+ 171	− 360	− 114	− 304	− 539	+ 171

$3.42	$6.29	$8.32	$3.73	$1.78	$5.32
− 2.11	+ 2.11	− 7.19	+ .53	+ 2.15	− 1.91

Read this line graph and answer the questions.

Lori works in a bakery. Every day, she makes bread.

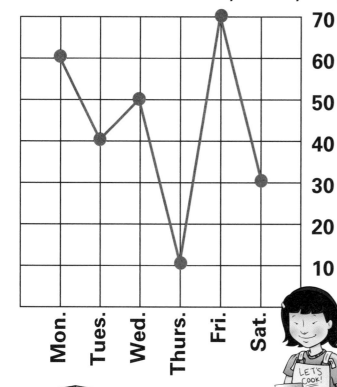

1. How many loaves of bread did Lori bake on Saturday?
   _____

2. On which two days did Lori bake 100 loaves of bread altogether?
   _____ and _____

3. On which day did Lori bake the most loaves? _____

4. On which day did Lori bake the fewest? _____

5. Name two other days that Lori baked 100 loaves of bread.
   _____ and _____

Read the poem; then do the activity below.

My Shadow

I have a little shadow that goes in and out with me,
And what can be the use of him is more than I can see.
He is very, very like me from the heels up to the head;
And I see him jump before me, when I jump into bed.

—Robert Louis Stevenson

1. What does your shadow do when you jump into bed?

_____

- -

_____

2. Who does your shadow look like?

_____

- -

_____

3. When do you see your shadow?

_____

- -

_____

4. What else can your shadow do besides jump?

_____

- -

_____

Write yes if the sentence is complete or no if it is not.

EXAMPLE:	A. Inside a large.	**No**
	B. Someone is walking on the sidewalk.	**Yes**
	1. I went to a movie last night.	_____
	2. We played in the park by.	_____
	3. Who is going to?	_____
	4. Today is my birthday.	_____
	5. Under the swing in front of the house.	_____
	6. Every Friday after school.	_____
	7. Did you enjoy reading that book?	_____
	8. Andy likes to play football.	_____

Air Friction

Which would hurt more if it fell on your head from a two-story building: a penny or a wad of paper? Which one would hit you first? What's air got to do with it?

Stuff You Need:

paper, penny

Here's What to Do:

1. Hold the penny and a smooth sheet of paper in front of you and higher than your head. Let them both fall at the same moment. What happens? Repeat this activity two more times.

2. Wad the paper into a tight ball. Hold the paper and coin in front of you and higher than your head and let them go at the same time. Repeat the experiment two more times.

3. Do the experiment again with sheets of paper that are wadded up, one loosely and one tightly.

4. Try different coins and other objects (make sure the objects you drop aren't breakable).

What's This All About?

Air has force, even though we can't see it. By wadding up the paper, you reduced the amount of force the air was able to put on the paper. We call this force **friction**.

Sometimes it's good to have a lot of air friction. You want a lot with a parachute, for example. Sometimes you don't want a lot of air friction, such as when you're trying to go fast in an airplane.

The more surface area an object has exposed to the air, the more frictional force the air can exert on the object. This activity shows the effect of air resistance on falling objects.

More Fun Ideas to Try:

1. Make a simple parachute that uses air friction to slow down a falling object. Use different materials (paper, fabrics, plastic bags) to make the parachute.

2. Find pictures of different types of cars. Look at their designs. Which cars do you think will cause less air friction?

Plaster Fossils

Fossils teach us about the plants and animals that have lived on Earth. Have you ever found a fossil? Did you wonder how it formed?

Stuff You Need:

adult   cardboard
craft stick   disposable plastic cup
modeling clay (1 stick)   plaster of Paris
stapler   water
plastic toy (a dinosaur would be cool!)

Here's What to Do:

1. Fill the cup with plaster of Paris (but don't add water—yet).

2. Have an adult help you cut a 1" x 8" cardboard strip. Roll the cardboard strip into a circle and staple the ends together.

3. Roll your clay into a ball. Flatten the clay into a pancake. It should be about 3 inches in diameter (across the middle) and about as thick as your pinky finger.

4. Press the toy into the middle of the clay pancake (do not make a hole all the way through the clay). Carefully take it out. The mark it leaves will become the fossil.

5. Place the cardboard strip around the clay near the edge; then push it into the clay. This is your mold.

6. Slowly add water to the plaster of Paris. Stir it until it looks like cake frosting. Quickly pour the plaster into the mold. The plaster should touch the edges of the cardboard.

7. Set the whole mold aside and clean up your mess. You will have a fossil in about one hour.

8. When the time is up, carefully peel the clay off the bottom of your mold. Peel away the cardboard. You now have a fossil!

What's This All About?

Fossils are impressions left by plants and animals that used to live on Earth. Dinosaurs would walk through soft mud, leaving footprints behind. Sometimes the mud hardened quickly enough to preserve the footprints. Other times, the footprints filled with sand, and then the sand hardened into rock, just like the plaster of Paris.

More Fun Ideas to Try:

1. Try making fossils of lots of different things: plants (such as a fern frond), seashells, paws from your pets, etc.

Answer Pages

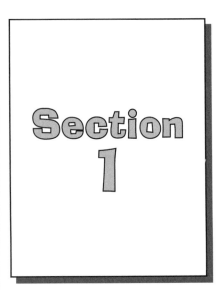

Section 1

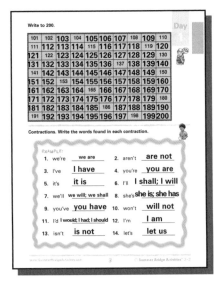

Page 3

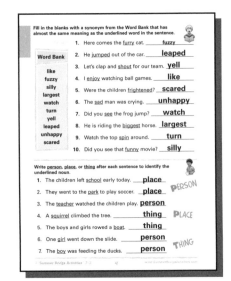

Page 4

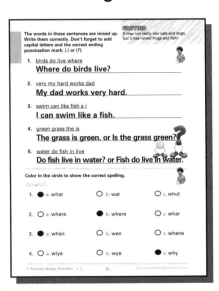

Page 5

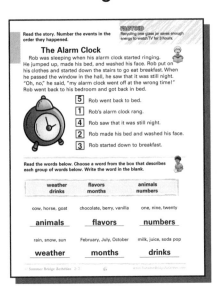

Page 6

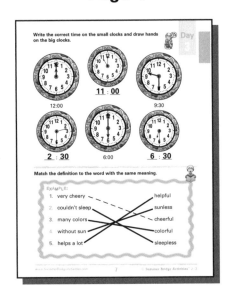

Page 7

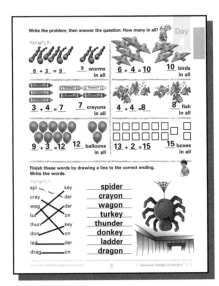

Page 8

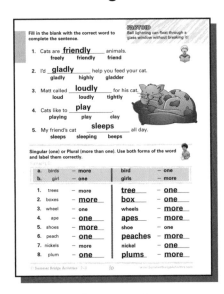

Page 9

Page 10

Page 11

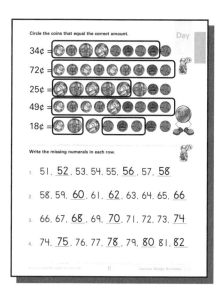

Circle the coins that equal the correct amount.

34¢
72¢
25¢
49¢
18¢

Write the missing numerals in each row.

1. 51, **52**, 53, 54, 55, **56**, 57, **58**
2. 58, 59, **60**, 61, **62**, 63, 64, 65, **66**
3. 66, 67, **68**, 69, **70**, 71, 72, 73, **74**
4. 74, **75**, 76, 77, **78**, 79, 80, 81, **82**

Page 12

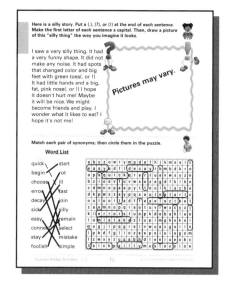

Here is a silly story. Put a (.), (?), or (!) at the end of each sentence. Make the first letter of each sentence a capital. Then, draw a picture of this "silly thing" the way you imagine it looks.

I saw a very silly thing. It had a very funny shape. It did not make any noise. It had spots that changed color and big feet with green toes(. or !) It had little hands and a big, fat, pink nose(. or !) I hope it doesn't hurt me! Maybe it will be nice. We might become friends and play. I wonder what it likes to eat? I hope it's not me!

Pictures may vary.

Match each pair of synonyms; then circle them in the puzzle.

Word List

quick — start
begin — rot
choose — ill
error — fast
decay — join
sick — silly
easy — remain
connect — select
stay — mistake
foolish — simple

Page 13

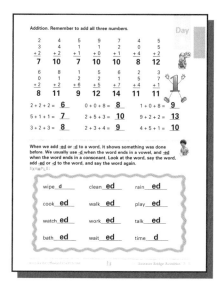

Addition. Remember to add all three numbers.

2	4	5	9	7	4	5
3	5	3	0	2	3	1
+2	+2	+1	+0	+1	+4	+2
7	**10**	**7**	**10**	**10**	**8**	**12**

6	8	1	6	2	3
0	1	2	1	5	3
+2	+2	+6	+5	+7	+4
8	**11**	**9**	**12**	**14**	**11**	**11**

2 + 2 + 2 = **6**   0 + 0 + 8 = **8**   1 + 0 + 8 = **9**
5 + 1 + 1 = **7**   2 + 5 + 3 = **10**   9 + 2 + 2 = **13**
3 + 2 + 3 = **8**   2 + 3 + 4 = **9**   4 + 5 + 1 = **10**

When we add -ed or -d to a word, it shows something was done before. We usually use -d when the word ends in a vowel, and -ed when the word ends in a consonant. Look at the word, say the word, add -ed or -d to the word, and say the word again.

wipe **d**   clean **ed**   rain **ed**
cook **ed**   walk **ed**   play **ed**
watch **ed**   work **ed**   talk **ed**
bath **ed**   wait **ed**   time **d**

Page 14

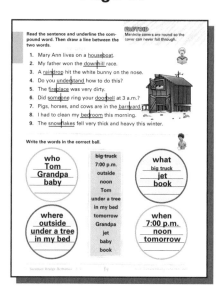

Read the sentence and underline the compound word. Then draw a line between the two words.

FASTOID Manhole covers are round so the cover can never fall through.

1. Mary Ann lives on a houseboat.
2. My father won the downhill race.
3. A raindrop hit the white bunny on the nose.
4. Do you understand how to do this?
5. The fireplace was very dirty.
6. Did someone ring your doorbell at 3 a.m.?
7. Pigs, horses, and cows are in the barnyard.
8. I had to clean my bedroom this morning.
9. The snowflakes fell very thick and heavy this winter.

Write the words in the correct ball.

who Tom Grandpa baby

big-truck 7:00 p.m. outside noon Tom under a tree in my bed tomorrow Grandpa jet baby book

what big truck jet book

where outside under a tree in my bed

when 7:00 p.m. noon tomorrow

Page 15

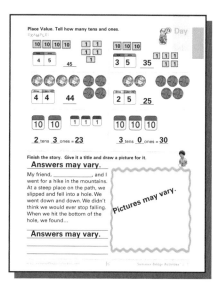

Place Value. Tell how many tens and ones.

4 5   45
3 5   35

4 4   44
2 5   25

2 tens 3 ones = 23
3 tens 0 ones = 30

Finish the story. Give it a title and draw a picture for it.

Answers may vary.

My friend, _____, and I went for a hike in the mountains. At a steep place on the path, we slipped and fell into a hole. We went down and down. We didn't think we would ever stop falling. When we hit the bottom of the hole, we found...

Answers may vary.

Pictures may vary.

Page 16

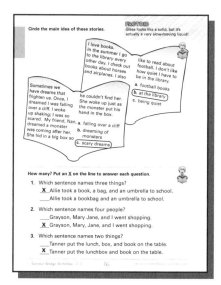

Circle the main idea of these stories.

FASTOID Glass looks like a solid, but it's actually a very slow-moving liquid.

I love books. In the summer I go to the library every other day. I check out books about horses and airplanes. I also like to read about football. I don't like how quiet I have to be in the library.
a. football books
b. at the library
c. being quiet

Sometimes we have dreams that frighten us. Once, I dreamed I was falling over a cliff. I woke up shaking; I was so scared. My friend, Nan, dreamed a monster was coming after her. She hid in a big box so he couldn't find her. She woke up just as the monster put his hand in the box.
a. falling over a cliff
b. dreaming of monsters
c. scary dreams

How many? Put an X on the line to answer each question.

1. Which sentence names three things?
   X Allie took a book, a bag, and an umbrella to school.
   ___ Allie took a bookbag and an umbrella to school.

2. Which sentence names four people?
   ___ Grayson, Mary Jane, and I went shopping.
   X Grayson, Mary Jane, and I went shopping.

3. Which sentence names two things?
   ___ Tanner put the lunch, box, and book on the table.
   X Tanner put the lunchbox and book on the table.

Page 17

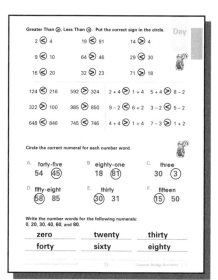

Greater Than (>), Less Than (<). Put the correct sign in the circle.

2 < 4   19 < 91   14 > 4
9 < 10   64 > 10   29 < 30
16 < 20   32 > 23   71 > 18

124 < 216   592 > 324   2 + 4 < 1 + 4   5 + 4 > 8 - 2
322 > 100   985 > 850   9 - 2 > 6 + 2   3 - 2 < 5 - 2
648 < 846   745 < 746   4 + 4 > 1 + 4   7 - 3 > 1 + 2

Circle the correct numeral for each number word.

A. forty-five   54 (45)
B. eighty-one   18 (81)
C. three   30 (3)
D. fifty-eight   (58) 85
E. thirty   (30) 31
F. fifteen   (15) 50

Write the number words for the following numerals: 0, 20, 30, 40, 60, and 80.

zero	twenty	thirty
forty	sixty	eighty

Page 18

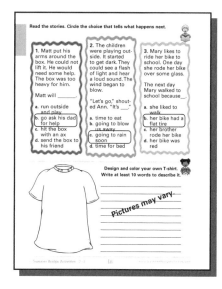

Read the stories. Circle the choice that tells what happens next.

1. Matt put his arms around the box. He could not lift it. He would need some help. The box was too heavy for him. Matt will _____.
   a. run outside and play
   b. go ask his dad for help
   c. hit the box with an ax
   d. send the box to his friend

2. The children were playing outside. It started to get dark. They could see a flash of light and hear a loud sound. The wind began to blow. "Let's go," shouted Ann. "It's ___."
   a. time to eat
   b. going to blow us away
   c. going to rain soon
   d. time for bed

3. Mary likes to ride her bike to school. One day she rode her bike over some glass. The next day Mary walked to school because___.
   a. she liked to walk
   b. her bike had a flat tire
   c. her brother rode her bike
   d. her bike was red

Design and color your own T-shirt. Write at least 10 words to describe it.

Pictures may vary.

Page 19

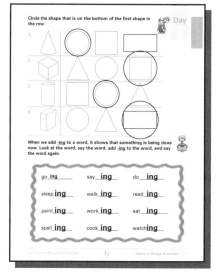

Circle the shape that is on the bottom of the first shape in the row.

When we add -ing to a word, it shows that something is being done now. Look at the word, say the word, add -ing to the word, and say the word again.

go **ing**   say **ing**   do **ing**
sleep **ing**   walk **ing**   read **ing**
paint **ing**   work **ing**   eat **ing**
spell **ing**   cook **ing**   watch **ing**

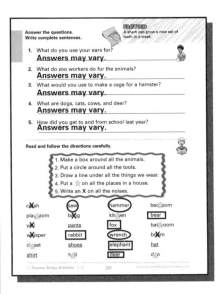

Page 20

Answer the questions. Write complete sentences.

FACTOID: A shark can grow a new set of teeth in a week.

1. What do you use your ears for?
Answers may vary.
2. What do zoo workers do for the animals?
Answers may vary.
3. What would you use to make a cage for a hamster?
Answers may vary.
4. What are dogs, cats, cows, and deer?
Answers may vary.
5. How did you get to and from school last year?
Answers may vary.

Read and follow the directions carefully.

1. Make a box around all the animals.
2. Put a circle around all the tools.
3. Draw a line under all the things we wear.
4. Put a ★ on all the places in a house.
5. Write an X on all the noises.

cXash | saw | hammer | bedXoom
playXoom | baXg | kitXen | bear
yXl | pants | fox | batXroom
wXisper | rabbit | wrench | boXm
closet | shoes | elephant | hat
shirt | hXl | deer | dXn

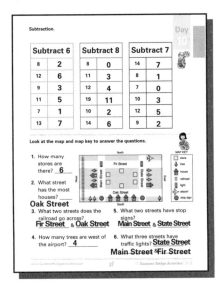

Page 21

Subtraction.

Subtract 6		Subtract 8		Subtract 7	
8	2	8	0	14	7
12	6	11	3	8	1
9	3	12	4	7	0
11	5	19	11	10	3
7	1	10	2	12	5
13	7	14	6	9	2

Look at the map and map key to answer the questions.

1. How many stores are there? **6**
2. What street has the most houses? **Oak Street**
3. What two streets does the railroad go across? **Fir Street** & **Oak Street**
4. How many trees are west of the airport? **4**
5. What two streets have stop signs? **Main Street** & **State Street**
6. What three streets have traffic lights? **Main Street** & **State Street** & **Fir Street**

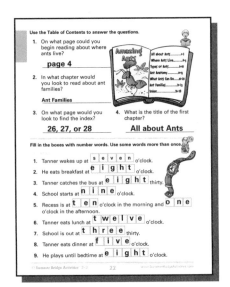

Page 22

Use the Table of Contents to answer the questions.

1. On what page could you begin reading about where ants live? **page 4**
2. In what chapter would you look to read about ant families? **Ant Families**
3. On what page would you look to find the index? **26, 27, or 28**
4. What is the title of the first chapter? **All about Ants**

Fill in the boxes with number words. Use some words more than once.

1. Tanner wakes up at **s e v e n** o'clock.
2. He eats breakfast at **e i g h t** o'clock.
3. Tanner catches the bus at **e i g h t** thirty.
4. School starts at **n i n e** o'clock.
5. Recess is at **t e n** o'clock in the morning and **o n e** o'clock in the afternoon.
6. Tanner eats lunch at **t w e l v e** o'clock.
7. School is out at **t h r e e** thirty.
8. Tanner eats dinner at **f i v e** o'clock.
9. He plays until bedtime at **e i g h t** o'clock.

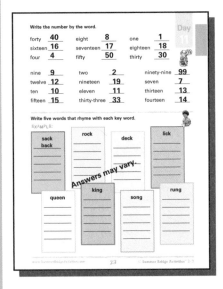

Page 23

Write the number by the word.

forty **40** | eight **8** | one **1**
sixteen **16** | seventeen **17** | eighteen **18**
four **4** | fifty **50** | thirty **30**

nine **9** | two **2** | ninety-nine **99**
twelve **12** | nineteen **19** | seven **7**
ten **10** | eleven **11** | thirteen **13**
fifteen **15** | thirty-three **33** | fourteen **14**

Write five words that rhyme with each key word.

EXAMPLE: sack / back

rock | deck | lick
queen | king | song | rung

Answers may vary.

Page 24

Tell what or whom the words mean.

FACTOID: The military salute came from knights raising their visors to the king.

EXAMPLE: The boys ran away. They ran to school. They = **boys**

1. Carla and I like horses. We ride them every day. them = **horses**
2. Grandma called today. She is coming to see us. She = **Grandma**
3. Joe would like to fly in a jet. He has never been in one. He = **Joe** one = **jet**
4. This summer, I am at camp. I like it here. here = **camp**
5. I lost my best umbrella. It is blue. It = **umbrella**
6. Lee has two dogs. They are both black. They = **dogs**

Read each sentence. Look carefully at the underlined word. Is it spelled right or wrong? Mark your answer.

		Right	Wrong
1.	Randy ate toast with jam on it.	●	○
2.	We wunt to the store for some candy.	○	●
3.	The dog will hund for his bone.	○	●
4.	We will plant our garden tonight.	●	○
5.	The keng asked the queen to come quickly.	○	●
6.	This is the ent of my story.	○	●
7.	I want my hair to grow very long.	●	○
8.	Think of a good name for a pet.	●	○

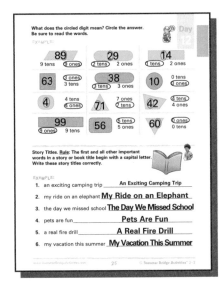

Page 25

What does the circled digit mean? Circle the answer. Be sure to read the words.

EXAMPLE:
89 — 9 tens / (9 ones)
29 — (2 tens) / 2 ones
14 — (1 tens) / 2 ones
63 — (3 ones) / 3 tens
38 — (3 tens) / 3 ones
10 — 1 tens / (0 ones)
4 — 4 tens / (4 ones)
71 — 7 ones / (7 tens)
42 — (4 tens) / 4 ones
99 — (9 ones) / 9 tens
56 — (5 tens) / 5 ones
60 — (0 ones) / 0 tens

Story Titles. Rule: The first and all other important words in a story or book title begin with a capital letter. Write these story titles correctly.

EXAMPLE:
1. an exciting camping trip — **An Exciting Camping Trip**
2. my ride on an elephant — **My Ride on an Elephant**
3. the day we missed school — **The Day We Missed School**
4. pets are fun — **Pets Are Fun**
5. a real fire drill — **A Real Fire Drill**
6. my vacation this summer — **My Vacation This Summer**

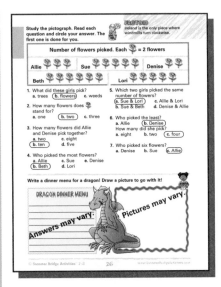

Page 26

Study the pictograph. Read each question and circle your answer. The first one is done for you.

FACTOID: Ireland is the only place where windmills turn clockwise.

Number of flowers picked. Each 🌸 = 2 flowers
Allie, Sue, Denise, Beth, Lori

1. What did these girls pick? a. trees (b. flowers) c. weeds
2. How many flowers does 🌸 stand for? a. one (b. two) c. three
3. How many flowers did Allie and Denise pick together? a. two b. eight (b. ten) d. five (c. four)
4. Who picked the most flowers? a. Allie c. Sue e. Denise (b. Beth) d. Lori
5. Which two girls picked the same number of flowers? (a. Sue & Lori) b. Allie & Lori c. Sue & Beth d. Denise & Allie
6. Who picked the least? a. Allie (b. Denise) How many did she pick? a. eight b. two c. four
7. Who picked six flowers? a. Denise b. Sue (e. Allie)

Write a dinner menu for a dragon! Draw a picture to go with it!

DRAGON DINNER MENU

Answers may vary. *Pictures may vary.*

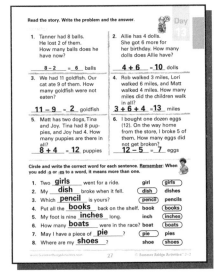

Page 27

Read the story. Write the problem and the answer.

1. Tanner had 8 balls. He lost 2 of them. How many balls does he have now? **8 – 2 = 6** balls
2. Allie has 4 dolls. She got 6 more for her birthday. How many dolls does Allie have? **4 + 6 = 10** dolls
3. We had 11 goldfish. Our cat ate 9 of them. How many goldfish were not eaten? **11 – 9 = 2** goldfish
4. Rob walked 3 miles, Lori walked 6 miles, and Matt walked 4 miles. How many miles did the children walk in all? **3 + 6 + 4 = 13** miles
5. Matt has two dogs, Tina and Joy. Tina had 8 puppies, and Joy had 4. How many puppies are there in all? **8 + 4 = 12** puppies
6. I bought one dozen eggs (12). On the way home from the store, I broke 5 of them. How many eggs did not get broken? **12 – 5 = 7** eggs

Circle and write the correct word for each sentence. Remember: When you add -s or -es to a word, it means more than one.

1. Two **girls** went for a ride. girl (girls)
2. My **dish** broke when it fell. (dish) dishes
3. Which **pencil** is yours? (pencil) pencils
4. Put all the **books** back on the shelf. book (books)
5. My foot is nine **inches** long. inch (inches)
6. My two **boats** were in the race? boat (boats)
7. May I have a piece of **pie**? (pie) pies
8. Where are my **shoes**? shoe (shoes)

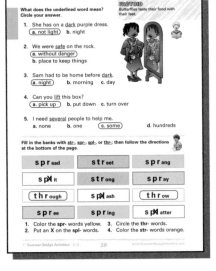

Page 28

What does the underlined word mean? Circle your answer.

FACTOID: Butterflies taste their food with their feet.

1. She has on a dark purple dress. (a. not light) b. night
2. We were safe on the rock. (a. without danger) b. place to keep things
3. Sam had to be home before dark. (a. night) b. morning c. day
4. Can you lift this box? (a. pick up) b. put down c. turn over
5. I need several people to help me. a. none b. one (c. some) d. hundreds

Fill in the banks with str-, spr-, spl-, or thr-; then follow the directions at the bottom of the page.

s p r ead | str eet | s p r ang
s pl it | str ong | s p r ay
th r ough | s pl ash | th r ow
s p r ee | s p r ing | s pl atter

1. Color the spr- words yellow.
2. Put an X on the spl- words.
3. Circle the thr- words.
4. Color the str- words orange.

Page 29

Write the missing sign (+, −, or =) in the circle.

6 ⊕ 3 = 9   12 ⊖ 6 = 6   4 ⊕ 2 = 2
4 + 3 ⊜ 7   14 ⊖ 1 = 15   12 ⊖ 2 = 10
9 ⊖ 3 = 6   4 ⊕ 4 = 10   14 − 7 ⊜ 7
4 ⊖ 1 = 3   7 − 3 ⊜ 4   3 ⊕ 9 = 10
8 ⊕ 4 = 12   9 ⊕ 2 = 11   11 ⊖ 2 = 9
7 + 3 ⊜ 10   10 ⊕ 3 = 13   12 − 4 ⊜ 8
10 ⊖ 8 = 2   3 ⊕ 8 = 11   10 + 2 ⊜ 12
4 ⊕ 4 = 8   6 + 4 ⊜ 10   0 + 9 ⊜ 9

Look at each base word and add the endings -er and -est.

	-er	-est
thin	thinner	thinnest
slim	slimmer	slimmest
big	bigger	biggest
hot	hotter	hottest
red	redder	reddest

Write the correct ending on each base word in the sentence.
1. That's the big**gest** cake on the table.
2. My cheeks are red**der** than your coat.
3. Jenna is slim**mer** than her brother.
4. Today is the hot**test** day we have had so far.
5. My sandwich is thin**ner** than yours.

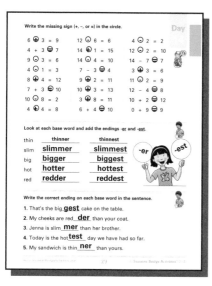

Page 30

FACTOID: An ostrich's eye is bigger than its brain.

Fill in the blanks. Use the words under the sentences.
1. We dressed in special **clothes** for the party. (cloth, clothes, clothed)
2. She turned on the **light** as we came in the room. (light, lighted, lighting)
3. We take our **tent** when we go camping. (lately, tent, rain)
4. We had **beans** for dinner. (banks, beaned, beans)
5. My bedroom is **blue**. (blow, blew, blue)

Look at the index below from the back of a book about flowers. Write the page where you could find information on each of the following flowers.
1. tulips **28**
2. pansies **31**
3. daisies **15**
4. roses **19**
5. zinnia **60**
6. lily **42**

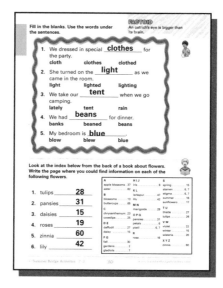

Page 31

Fill in the missing numbers.

300 301 302 303 304 305 306 307 308 309
310 311 312 313 314 315 316 317 318 319
489 490 491 492 493 494 495 496 497 498
202 203 204 205 206 207 208 209 210 211
595 596 597 598 599 600 601 602 603 604

Circle the words that should have a capital letter. Put a period (.) or question mark (?) at the end of each sentence.
1. rachel lives in new york city.
2. i live in salt lake city, utah.
3. where do you live?
4. mr. brown is my best neighbor.
5. was easter in april this year?
6. my mother shops at smith's market.
7. where is dallas, texas?
8. look what i've got.
9. children say "trick or treat" on halloween.
10. do you like christmas or thanksgiving better?

Page 32

Fill in the blanks. Use the words in the box.

FACTOID: Frogs can launch themselves over 20 times their own body length.

Box: trade, summer, cowboy, dry, ambulance, brought

1. Do you like to go swimming in the **summer**?
2. My little brother wants to be a **cowboy** when he grows up.
3. The **ambulance** made a loud noise as it passed us.
4. I'll **trade** my banana for your orange.
5. Sammy **brought** a big snake to school in a box.
6. The ground has not been **dry** this summer.

Use the dictionary entry below to answer the questions.

germ (jûrm) n. 1. disease-producing microbe. 2. a bud or seed.

1. What part of speech is germ? **noun**
2. Which definition of germ deals with growing plants? **two**
3. Would the word germinate come before or after the word germ in the dictionary? **after**
4. Use the word germ in a sentence. **Answers will vary.**

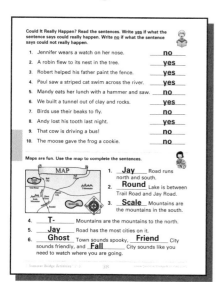

Section 2

Page 37

Build the pyramid. Write the answers in the stones.

3 +1 4 −1 3 +2 5
5 −2 3 +4 7 −2 5 +4 9 −4 5
9 −6 3 −3 0 +8 8 +2 10 −7 3
12 −8 4 +6 10 −6 2 −4 4 +9 13 +2 15 −5 10

Some words end with two of the same consonant.

off, fell, dress, stiff, shall, class, stuff, glass, ball, mitt, hill

1. Write the word from the box that rhymes with these words.
bell — **fell**
fill — **hill**
puff — **stuff**

2. Fill in the missing word or words. Use words from the box.
Our **class** will put on a play for you.
I **fell** down and hurt my hand. Answers may vary.
Put some milk in my **glass**, please.
Grab your **mitt**, and let's play **ball**.
The man is on top of the **hill**.
Stand still, and I will show you my new **dress**.

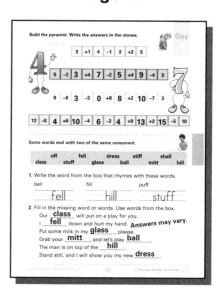

Page 38

Could It Really Happen? Read the sentences. Write yes if what the sentence says could really happen. Write no if what the sentence says could not really happen.
1. Jennifer wears a watch on her nose. **no**
2. A robin flew to its nest in the tree. **yes**
3. Robert helped his father paint the fence. **yes**
4. Paul saw a striped cat swim across the river. **yes**
5. Mandy eats her lunch with a hammer and saw. **no**
6. We built a tunnel out of clay and rocks. **yes**
7. Birds use their beaks to fly. **no**
8. Andy lost his tooth last night. **yes**
9. That cow is driving a bus! **no**
10. The moose gave the frog a cookie. **no**

Maps are fun. Use the map to complete the sentences.
1. **Jay** Road runs north and south.
2. **Round** Lake is between Trail Road and Jay Road.
3. **Scale** Mountains are the mountains in the south.
4. **T-** Mountains are the mountains to the north.
5. **Jay** Road has the most cities on it.
6. **Ghost** Town sounds spooky, **Friend** City sounds friendly, and **Fall** City sounds like you need to watch where you are going.

Page 39

Add or subtract.

84 − 42 = 42   37 − 13 = 24   69 + 20 = 89   18 − 4 = 14   57 + 21 = 78   70 + 30 = 100   87 − 36 = 51
22 − 16 = 6   24 − 11 = 13   10 − 10 = 0   23 + 12 = 35   26 + 22 = 48   35 + 33 = 68   99 − 34 = 65
43 + 43 = 86   91 + 6 = 97   15 − 9 = 6   12 + 2 = 14   49 − 38 = 11   16 + 3 = 19   287 − 12 = 275

Read the words in each group and put them in the correct order. Place a period (.) or a question mark (?) at the end of each sentence. Read your sentence.

1 It is fun   3 Allie went?   3 bones.
3 new friends.   1 know where   1 My dog
2 to make   2 Do you   2 can eat

1 Ms. Hansen gave   2 car passed   2 Tanner are
3 their papers.   1 A green   1 Grayson and
2 the children   3 us.   3 brothers.

1 Matt has   3 kinds of cookies.   3 love me.
3 of cars.   1 Denise ate   2 and mom
2 four kinds   2 four different   1 My dad

Page 40

Read this paragraph; then follow the directions.

Denise likes to do many different things in the summer. Denise likes to sleep until eight o'clock. After she gets up, she likes to help her mother work in the garden for a while. Every day Denise likes to read and play with her friends. She likes to go swimming and hiking with her brothers. And most of all, she likes to ride her horse.

1. Underline the topic sentence.
2. Whom does Denise go swimming with? Circle your answer.
3. Put an X on the time Denise gets up.
4. What do you think would be a good name for Denise's horse? **Answers will vary.**
5. Name two things that might be growing in Denise's garden. **Answers will vary.**

Crossword Puzzle. Read the sentences. Choose a word from the box below to complete the puzzle.

Box: supper, camera, rake, cheese, agree, meat, microphone

1. You talk into this to make your voice loud.
2. You can eat this.
3. You take pictures with this.
4. You eat this at night.
5. People and mice like this.
6. My friend and I ___ on most things.
7. You do this to the leaves on your lawn.

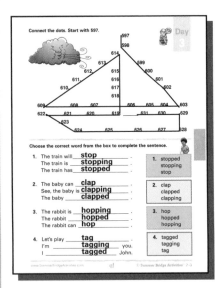

Page 41

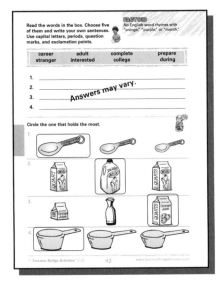

Page 42

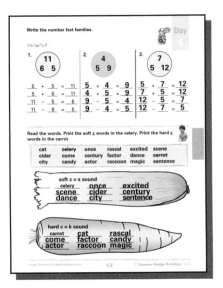

Page 43

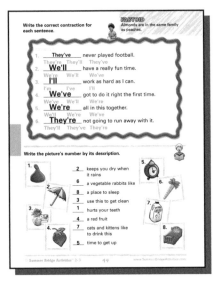

Page 44

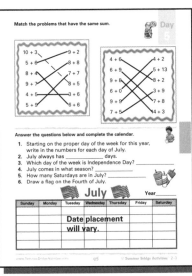

Page 45

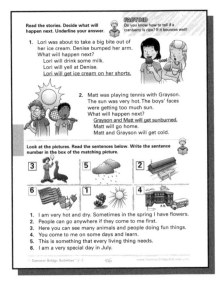

Page 46

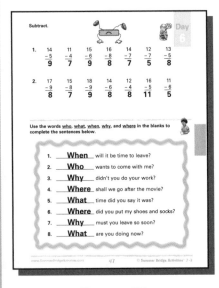

Page 47

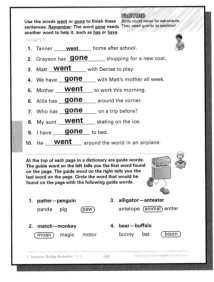

Page 48

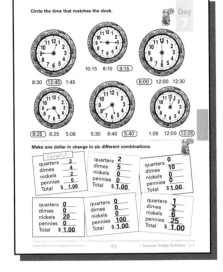

Page 49

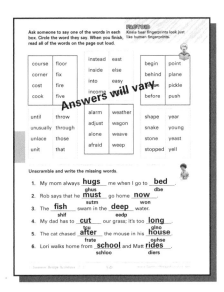

Page 50

Ask someone to say one of the words in each box. Circle the word they say. When you finish, read all of the words on the page out loud.

FACTOID Koala bear fingerprints look just like human fingerprints.

course	floor
corner	fix
cost	fire
cook	five

instead	east
inside	else
into	easy
income	
before	push

begin	point
behind	plane
	pickle

Answers will vary.

until	throw
unusually	through
unlace	those
unit	that

alarm	weather
adjust	wagon
alone	weave
afraid	weep

shape	year
snake	young
stone	yeast
stopped	yell

Unscramble and write the missing words.

1. My mom always **hugs** me when I go to **bed** .
   ghus / dbe
2. Rob says that he **must** go home **now** .
   sutm / won
3. The **fish** swam in the **deep** water.
   shif / eedp
4. My dad has to **cut** our grass; it's too **long** .
   tcu / glno
5. The cat chased **after** the mouse in his **house** .
   frate / ouhse
6. Lori walks home from **school** and Matt **rides** .
   schloo / diers

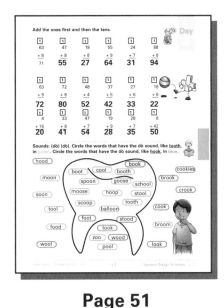

Page 51

Add the ones first and then the tens.

63	47	19	55	24	88
+ 8	+ 8	+ 8	+ 9	+ 7	+ 6
71	55	27	64	31	94

63	72	48	37	27	16
+ 9	+ 8	+ 4	+ 5	+ 6	+ 6
72	80	52	42	33	22

4	33	47	19	28	8
+ 16	+ 8	+ 7	+ 9	+ 7	+ 42
20	41	54	28	35	50

Sounds: (o͞o) (o͝o). Circle the words that have the o͞o sound, like **tooth**, in green. Circle the words that have the o͝o sound, like **hook**, in blue.

hood, moon, boot, cool, booth, book, cookies, spoon, goose, school, brook, soon, moose, hoop, stool, crook, scoop, tooth, tool, balloon, foot, stood, cook, food, took, broom, wool, zoo, wood, look, pool

---

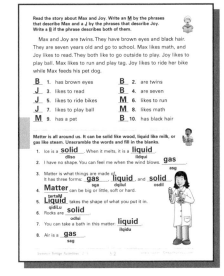

Page 52

Read the story about Max and Joy. Write an M by the phrases that describe Max and a J by the phrases that describe Joy. Write a B if the phrase describes both of them.

Max and Joy are twins. They have brown eyes and black hair. They are seven years old and go to school. Max likes math, and Joy likes to read. They both like to go outside to play. Max likes to run and play tag. Joy likes to ride her bike while Max feeds his pet dog.

B 1. has brown eyes	**B** 2. are twins
J 3. likes to read	**B** 4. are seven
J 5. likes to ride bikes	**M** 6. likes to run
J 7. likes to play ball	**M** 8. likes math
M 9. has a pet	**B** 10. has black hair

Matter is all around us. It can be solid like wood, liquid like milk, or gas like steam. Unscramble the words and fill in the blanks.

1. Ice is a **solid** . When it melts, it is a **liquid** .
   dliso / ildqui
2. I have no shape. You can feel me when the wind blows. **gas**
   asg
3. Matter is what things are made of. It has three forms: **gas** , **liquid** , and **solid** .
   sga / dqilul / osdil
4. **Matter** can be big or little, soft or hard.
   tertaM
5. **Liquid** takes the shape of what you put it in.
   qidiLu
6. Rocks are **solid** .
   odlsi
7. You can take a bath in this matter. **liquid**
   ilqidu
8. Air is a **gas** .
   sag

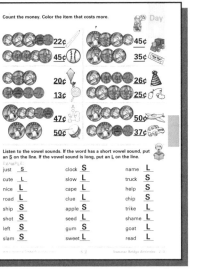

Page 53

Count the money. Color the item that costs more.

22¢ / 45¢
45¢ / 35¢
20¢ / 26¢
13¢ / 25¢
47¢ / 50¢
50¢ / 37¢

Listen to the vowel sounds. If the word has a short vowel sound, put an S on the line. If the vowel sound is long, put an L on the line.

EXAMPLE:
just **S**

cute **L**	clock **S**	name **L**
nice **L**	slow **L**	truck **S**
road **L**	cape **L**	help **S**
ship **S**	clue **L**	chip **S**
shot **S**	apple **S**	trike **L**
left **S**	seed **L**	shame **L**
slam **S**	gum **S**	goat **L**
	sweet **L**	read **L**

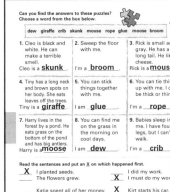

Page 54

Can you find the answers to these puzzles? Choose a word from the box below.

dew giraffe crib skunk mouse rope glue moose broom

1. Cleo is black and white. He can make a terrible smell. Cleo is a **skunk** .
2. Sweep the floor with me. I'm a **broom** .
3. Rick is small and gray. He has a long tail. He likes cheese. Rick is a **mouse** .
4. Tiny has a long neck and brown spots on her body. She eats leaves off the trees. Tiny is a **giraffe** .
5. You can stick things together with me. I am **glue** .
6. You can tie things up with me. I can be thick or thin. I'm a **rope** .
7. Harry lives in the forest by a pond. He eats grass on the bottom of the pond and has big antlers. Harry is a **moose** .
8. You can find me on the grass in the morning on cool days. I am **dew** .
9. Babies sleep in me. I have four legs, but I can't walk. I'm a **crib** .

Read the sentences and put an X on which happened first.
- **X** I planted seeds.
  The flowers grew.
- I did my work.
  X I must do my work.
- Katie spent all of her money.
  X Katie has a lot of money.
- **X** Kirt starts his car.
  Kirt drives his car.
- I brushed my teeth.
  X I put toothpaste on my brush.
- **X** Our snowman is tall.
  Our snowman melted.
- I put my shoes on.
  X I put on my socks.
- Mom baked a cake.
  X I ate a piece of cake.

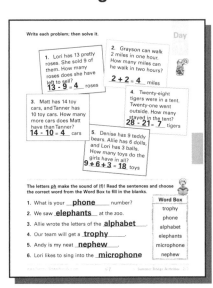

Page 55

Add.

32	28	70	44	57	26
11	14	99	2	32	33
+ 19	+ 4	+ 12	+ 38	+ 89	+ 44
62	46	181	84	178	103

81	22	67	81	74	6
38	9	45	8	33	24
+ 64	+ 19	+ 15	+ 8	+ 17	+ 36
183	50	127	97	124	66

Put these words in alphabetical order. They are r-controlled vowel words. Can you spell them all?

her	card	jerk	turn	march
word	are	burn	more	store
bird	third	dark	part	first

1. **are**   6. **first**   11. **part**
2. **bird**   7. **her**   12. **store**
3. **burn**   8. **jerk**   13. **third**
4. **card**   9. **march**   14. **turn**
5. **dark**   10. **more**   15. **word**

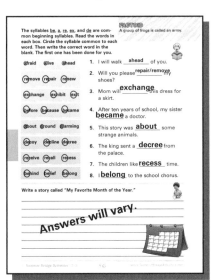

Page 56

The syllables be, a, re, ex, and de are common beginning syllables. Read the words in each box. Circle the syllable common to each word. Then write the correct word in the blank. The first one has been done for you.

FACTOID A group of frogs is called an army.

afraid alive ahead
remove repair renew
exchange exhibit exit
before because became
about around alarming
decoy decline decree
receive recall recess
behind belief belong

1. I will walk **ahead** of you.
2. Will you please **repair/renew** my shoes?
3. Mom will **exchange** this dress for a skirt.
4. After ten years of school, my sister **became** a doctor.
5. This story is **about** some strange animals.
6. The king sent a **decree** from the palace.
7. The children like **recess** time.
8. I **belong** to the school chorus.

Write a story called "My Favorite Month of the Year."

Answers will vary.

Page 57

Write each problem; then solve it.

1. Lori has 13 pretty roses. She sold 9 of them. How many roses does she have left to sell?
   13 - 9 = 4 roses
2. Grayson can walk 2 miles in one hour. How many miles can he walk in two hours?
   2 + 2 = 4 miles
3. Matt has 14 toy cars, and Tanner has 10 toy cars. How many more cars does Matt have than Tanner?
   14 - 10 = 4 cars
4. Twenty-eight tigers were in a tent. Twenty-one went outside. How many stayed in the tent?
   28 - 21 = 7 tigers
5. Denise has 9 teddy bears. Allie has 6 dolls, and Lori has 3 balls. How many toys do the girls have in all?
   9 + 6 + 3 = 18 toys

The letters ph make the sound of (f)! Read the sentences and choose the correct word from the Word Box to fill in the blanks.

1. What is your **phone** number?
2. We saw **elephants** at the zoo.
3. Allie wrote the letters of the **alphabet** .
4. Our team will get a **trophy** .
5. Andy is my neat **nephew** .
6. Lori likes to sing into the **microphone** .

Word Box
trophy
phone
alphabet
elephants
microphone
nephew

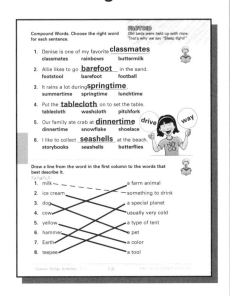

Page 58

Compound Words. Choose the right word for each sentence.

FACTOID Old beds were held up with rope. That's why we say "Sleep tight!"

1. Denise is one of my favorite **classmates**
   classmates rainbows buttermilk
2. Allie likes to go **barefoot** in the sand.
   footstool barefoot football
3. It rains a lot during **springtime** .
   summertime springtime lunchtime
4. Put the **tablecloth** on to set the table.
   tablecloth washcloth pitchfork
5. Our family ate crab at **dinnertime** .
   dinnertime snowflake shoelace
6. I like to collect **seashells** at the beach.
   storybooks seashells butterflies

Draw a line from the word in the first column to the words that best describe it.
EXAMPLE:
1. milk — something to drink
2. ice cream — usually very cold
3. dog — a pet
4. cow — a farm animal
5. yellow — a color
6. hammer — a tool
7. Earth — a special planet
8. teepee — a type of tent

Page 59

Write the temperature in the first blank. Write warm or cold in the second blank.

1. 10 °F — cold
2. 90 °F — warm
3. 20 °F — cold
4. 70 °F — warm

Put the words from the box below into the correct categories.

Box: cow, blocks, rabbit, beans, bread, monkey, ball, sled, kite, horse, meat, donkey, corn, cherry, lion, potatoes, train, doll

Animals
1. cow
2. rabbit
3. monkey
4. horse
5. donkey
6. lion

Toys
1. blocks
2. ball
3. sled
4. kite
5. train
6. doll

Foods
1. beans
2. bread
3. meat
4. corn
5. cherry
6. potatoes

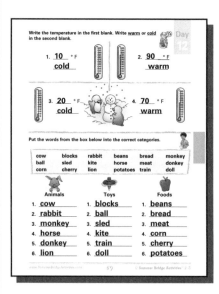

Page 60

Read the story and the summaries. Circle the best summary.

FACTOID: Penguins have an organ that can change salt water into fresh water.

Matt loved to play in the water. Every time it rained, he would run outside to play in the puddles. He would splash water on his dog and the neighbor's cat. He would even splash water on anyone who came near. His friends would not play with him because he always got them wet. One day, a big truck went by and splashed water all over Matt. He got so wet he decided not to splash people anymore.

1. Matt liked to play in puddles of water. He got wet. He didn't splash anymore.
2. Matt liked to play in puddles of water. He splashed on animals and people. One day a truck splashed him. He stopped splashing others.

A thesaurus is a book that includes synonyms of words. You can use a thesaurus to make your writing more interesting. Look at this page from a thesaurus. Answer the questions below.

sad (adj): unhappy, down, dismal, morose, miserable, cheerless, gloomy, forlorn, dejected, glum, depressed

said (v): spoke, repeated, harped, yelled, whispered, echoed, bellowed, whined, shouted, told, sang, hammered, mentioned

1. Are the synonyms for the entry word in alphabetical order? **No**
2. What does the (adj) after the word sad tell you about the word? **It's an adjective.**
3. Rewrite this sentence using a synonym for the word sad: The boy was feeling sad because he lost his puppy. **Answers will vary.**

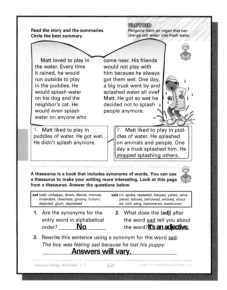

Page 61

Brooke saves buttons. Below are some she has collected. Read and solve the riddles. Write the letter of the button that matches the clues.

A   B   C   D   E   F

1. I do not have corners. I have 2 lines of symmetry. Which button am I? **E**
2. I am not round. I have more than 4 corners. I show symmetry. Which button am I? **D**
3. I have 4 corners. I have 2 lines of symmetry. Two sides are longer than the other 2 sides. Which button am I? **F**
4. Now you write clues for the rest of the buttons. Can your friends and family guess? **Answers will vary.**

Days of the week begin with capital letters. Fill in the blanks with the names of the days. Look at a calendar to help you spell them.

1. School days are **Monday**, **Tuesday**, **Wednesday**, **Thursday**, and **Friday**.
2. On what day of the week does Thanksgiving always fall? **Thursday**
3. Write the names of the days that have six letters: **Friday**, **Monday**, and **Sunday**.
4. What day comes after Friday? **Saturday**
5. Which days have eight letters? **Thursday** and **Saturday**
6. **Tuesday** has seven letters, and **Wednesday** has nine.

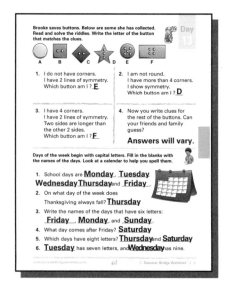

Page 62

Word Referents. Read the sentences. Draw a circle around the word or words that the underlined word stands for.

FACTOID: Maine is the only state with a one-syllable name.

1. If you'll be home (Friday), I'll see you then.
2. The (fruit) is really good; it tastes sweet.
3. (Joe and Henry) ran fast; they won the race.
4. When we found the (park), Dad said, "Let's eat here."
5. (Mary) plays the piano; she plays very well.
6. I watered the (flowers) and put them on the bench.
7. Danny took the dog (outside); he left the cat there, too.
8. The (fish) swam in the pond; it ate a bug.

Circle all the small words you can find in these words. **Answers may vary.**

EXAMPLE: toward, forest

1. statement
2. infant
3. storage
4. spend
5. behind
6. million
7. bonnet
8. kittens
9. identify
10. penmanship
11. twinkled
12. balloon
13. friend
14. carpet
15. rabbit
16. spring
17. pinch
18. chocolate
19. kingdom
20. canyon
21. sentence

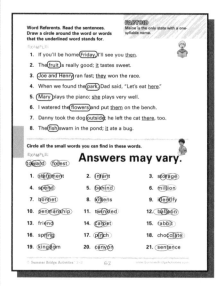

Page 63

Subtract.

Row 1: 13, 49, 45, 8, 46, 25
Row 2: 56, 59, 17, 39, 14, 19
Row 3: 75, 15, 46, 19, 39, 24

Look at the geometric solids. Each side is called a face. Write the number of faces each solid has.

1. cube — 6 faces
2. triangular prism — 2 faces, 3 faces
3. rectangular prism — 2 faces, 4 faces
4. rectangular prism — 2 faces, 4 faces

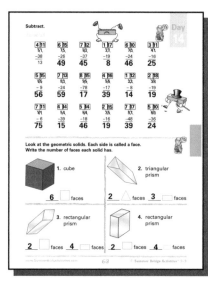

Page 64

Read each sentence and mark the correct one. Pay close attention to the commas.

FACTOID: Crocodiles can't move their tongues.

1. Denise wanted five things in her lunch.
   - **X** Denise got an apple, cake, an orange, carrots, and candy for her lunch.
   - ___ Denise got an applecake, an orange, carrots, and candy for her lunch.
2. Grayson saw three children at the park.
   - **X** Alex Lee, Henry, and John were playing ball.
   - ___ Alex, Lee, Henry, and John were playing at the park.
3. Lori has four things in her room.
   - ___ She has a basketball, a teddy bear, and a book.
   - **X** She has a basket, a ball, a teddy bear, and a book.

Write these summer words in the boxes. Make sure they fit.

swimming, fishing, baseball, football, camping, vacation

Crossword: play, swimming, baseball, skiing, camping, fishing, football, biking, vacation, biking, fun, play, (water) skiing

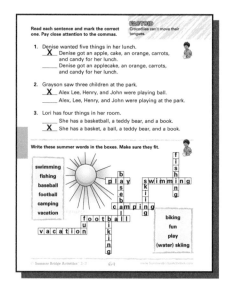

Page 65

Count the money. Write in the amount for each line.

1. 88¢
2. 77¢
3. 62¢
4. 51¢
5. 75¢

Change the order of each telling sentence to form a question. Remember the question mark.

EXAMPLE: The busy mailman is leaving. → Is the busy mailman leaving?

1. The old man is Gary's grandfather.
2. Apples are red, round, and juicy.
3. She will ride her shiny, new bike.
4. I am going to ride a black horse.

Answers will vary.

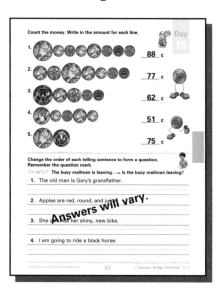

Page 66

Fill in the blank with the correct word to complete each sentence.

1. My grandma reached the **age** of 100 years. (ant, age, ape)
2. Denise likes to **play** beauty salon. (peel, plate, play)
3. My mom put on a **lovely** dress. (biggest, lovely, lately)
4. The grass turns green in the **spring**. (sprang, spring, sprung)
5. The **light** was shining in my eyes. (bright, flight, light)
6. A horse kicks with its **hind** legs. (blind, hind, mind)
7. The fence was made of **wire**. (wire, tire, fire)
8. I will pay the **fare** so I can ride the bus. (rare, square, fare)

Follow the directions to make a picture.

1. Draw a line from 3 to 5.
2. Draw a line from 3 to C to 9.
3. Draw a line from 3 to D.
4. Draw a line from D to Z to 5.
5. Draw a line from Z to 9.
6. Draw a line from 3 to R to D.
7. Draw a line from 3 to Z.
8. Color and add things you would take camping.

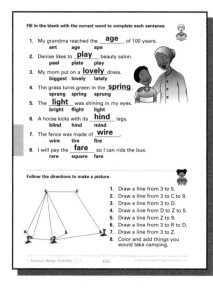

Page 67

Draw two straight lines to divide the square so each area totals...

11   12

Abbreviations. To abbreviate a word means to shorten it. Match these abbreviations and words.

EXAMPLE:
- December — Dec.
- Doctor — Dr.
- Thursday — Thur.
- ounce — oz.
- January — Jan.

- Mister — Mr.
- October — Oct.
- ft. — foot
- Ave. — Avenue
- U.S.A. — United States of America

- yd. — yard
- March — Mar.
- Jr. — Junior
- inch — in.
- Wednesday — Wed.

- Saturday — Sat.
- Senior — Sr.
- Monday — Mon.
- Captain — Capt.
- street — St.

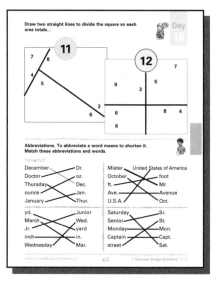

Page 68

Read the sentences. Put a (.), (?), or (!) at the end of each sentence.

1. It will soon be the first day of school. or !
2. Will Judy ride her bike to school this year ?
3. Have you had a fun summer vacation ?
4. My family went on a camping trip to the beach .
5. Ann's sister will be starting school this year .
6. What day will school start for you ?
7. Do you know the name of your new teacher ?
8. She will learn to be a teacher .
9. Have you gone anywhere before ?
10. Have fun !

Look at the parts of the bird, and then write them in alphabetical order.

crown, eye, beak, back, throat, wings, breast, belly, tail, feet

1. back
2. beak
3. belly
4. breast
5. crown
6. eye
7. feet
8. tail
9. throat
10. wings

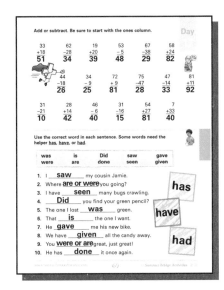

Page 69

Add or subtract. Be sure to start with the ones column.

33 +18 = 51	62 -28 = 34	19 +20 = 39	53 - 5 = 48	67 -38 = 29	58 +24 = 82
44 -18 = 26	34 - 9 = 25	72 + 9 = 81	75 -47 = 28	47 -14 = 33	81 +11 = 92
31 -21 = 10	28 +14 = 42	46 - 6 = 40	31 -16 = 15	54 +27 = 81	7 +33 = 40

Use the correct word in each sentence. Some words need the helper has, have, or had.

was, were, is, are, Did, done, saw, seen, gave, given

1. I **saw** my cousin Jamie.
2. Where **are or were** you going?
3. I have **seen** many bugs crawling.
4. **Did** you find your green pencil?
5. The one I lost **was** green.
6. That **is** the one I want.
7. He **gave** me his new bike.
8. We have **given** all the candy away.
9. You **were or are** great, just great!
10. He has **done** it once again.

has, have, had

Page 70

Change the spelling of the underlined words to make them plural.

FACTOID: Giraffes have long tongues—they can lick their own eyes!

mice, elves, leaves, knives, feet, teeth, geese, men

1. one man or two **men**
2. one tooth or three **teeth**
3. one leaf or four **leaves**
4. one goose or five **geese**
5. one knife or two **knives**
6. one mouse or six **mice**
7. one elf or four **elves**
8. one foot or nine **feet**

Pretend you live in a tree house! Write a story describing what it's like to live in your tree house:

Answers will vary.

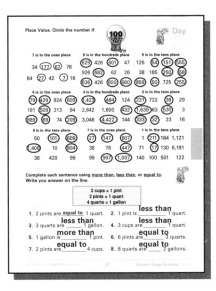

Page 71

Place Value. Circle the number if:

7 is in the ones place / 6 is in the hundreds place / 5 is in the tens place

9 is in the ones place / 4 is in the hundreds place / 8 is in the tens place

0 is in the tens place / 7 is in the tens place / 1 is in the ones place

Complete each sentence using more than, less than, or equal to. Write you answer on the line.

2 cups = 1 pint
2 pints = 1 quart
4 quarts = 1 gallon

1. 2 pints are **equal to** 1 quart.
2. 1 pint is **less than** 1 quart.
3. 3 quarts is **less than** 1 gallon.
4. 3 cups is **less than** 1 quart.
5. 1 gallon is **more than** 1 pint.
6. 6 pints are **equal to** 3 quarts.
7. 2 pints are **equal to** 4 cups.
8. 8 quarts are **equal to** 2 gallons.

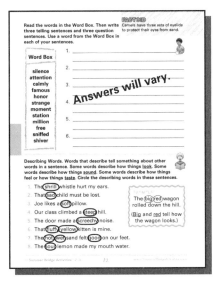

Page 72

Read the words in the Word Box. Then write three telling sentences and three question sentences. Use a word from the Word Box in each of your sentences.

FACTOID: Camels have three sets of eyelids to protect their eyes from sand.

Word Box: silence, attention, calmly, famous, honor, strange, moment, station, million, free, sniffed, shiver

1.
2.
3.
4.
5.
6.

Answers will vary.

Describing Words. Words that describe tell something about other words in a sentence. Some words describe how things look. Some words describe how things sound. Some words describe how things feel or how things taste. Circle the describing words in these sentences.

1. The shrill whistle hurt my ears.
2. That sad child must be lost.
3. Joe likes a soft pillow.
4. Our class climbed a steep hill.
5. The door made a screechy noise.
6. That fluffy yellow kitten is mine.
7. The hot wet sand felt good on our feet.
8. The sour lemon made my mouth water.

EXAMPLE: The big red wagon rolled down the hill. (Big and red tell how the wagon looks.)

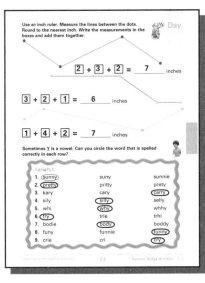

Page 73

Use an inch ruler. Measure the lines between the dots. Round to the nearest inch. Write the measurements in the boxes and add them together.

2 + 3 + 2 = 7 inches

3 + 2 + 1 = 6 inches

1 + 4 + 2 = 7 inches

Sometimes Y is a vowel. Can you circle the word that is spelled correctly in each row?

1. sunny / suny / sunnie
2. pretty / pritty / prety
3. kary / cary / carry
4. sily / silly / selly
5. whi / why / whhy
6. try / trie / trhi
7. bodie / body / boddy
8. funy / funnie / funny
9. crie / cri / cry

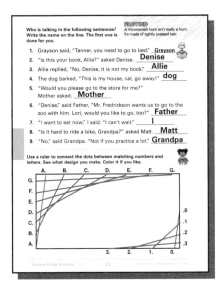

Page 74

Who is talking in the following sentences? Write the name on the line. The first one is done for you.

FACTOID: A rhinoceros's horn isn't really a horn. It's made of tightly pressed hair.

1. Grayson said, "Tanner, you need to go to bed." **Grayson**
2. "Is this your book, Allie?" asked Denise. **Denise**
3. Allie replied, "No, Denise, it is not my book." **Allie**
4. The dog barked, "This is my house, cat, go away!" **dog**
5. "Would you please go to the store for me?" Mother asked. **Mother**
6. "Denise," said Father, "Mr. Fredrickson wants us to go to the zoo with him. Lori, would you like to go, too?" **Father**
7. "I want to eat now," I said. "I can't wait." **I**
8. "Is it hard to ride a bike, Grandpa?" asked Matt. **Matt**
9. "No," said Grandpa. "Not if you practice a lot." **Grandpa**

Use a ruler to connect the dots between matching numbers and letters. See what design you make. Color it if you like.

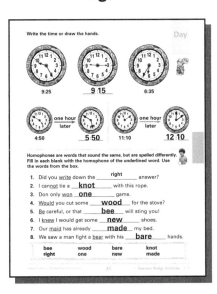

Page 75

Write the time or draw the hands.

9:25, 9:15, 6:35

4:50 one hour later 5:50, 11:10 one hour later 12:10

Homophones are words that sound the same, but are spelled differently. Fill in each blank with the homophone of the underlined word. Use the words from the box.

1. Did you write down the **right** answer?
2. I cannot tie a **knot** with this rope.
3. Don only won **one** game.
4. Would you cut some **wood** for the stove?
5. Be careful, or that **bee** will sting you!
6. I knew I would get some **new** shoes.
7. Our maid has already **made** my bed.
8. We saw a man fight a bear with his **bare** hands.

bee, wood, bare, knot, right, one, new, made

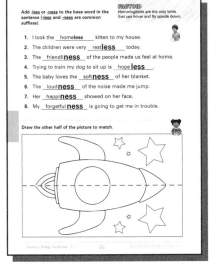

Page 76

Add -less or -ness to the base word in the sentence (-less and -ness are common suffixes).

FACTOID: Hummingbirds are the only birds that can hover and fly upside down.

1. I took the **homeless** kitten to my house.
2. The children were very **restless** today.
3. The **friendliness** of the people made us feel at home.
4. Trying to train my dog to sit up is **hopeless**.
5. The baby loves the **softness** of her blanket.
6. The **loudness** of the noise made me jump.
7. Her **happiness** showed on her face.
8. My **forgetfulness** is going to get me in trouble.

Draw the other half of the picture to match.

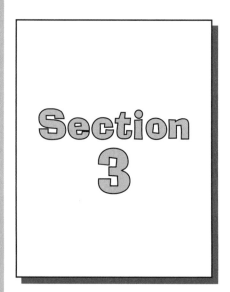

Section 3

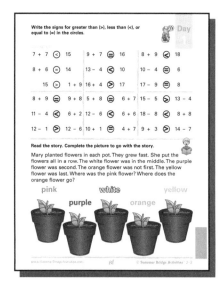

Page 81

Write the signs for greater than (>), less than (<), or equal to (=) in the circles.

7 + 7 < 15	9 + 7 = 16	8 + 9 < 18
8 + 6 = 14	13 − 4 < 10	10 − 4 = 6
15 > 1 + 9	16 + 4 > 17	17 − 9 = 8
8 + 9 = 9 + 8	5 + 8 = 6 + 7	15 − 5 > 13 − 4
11 − 4 < 6 + 2	12 − 6 < 6 + 7	18 − 8 < 8 + 8
12 − 1 > 12 − 6	10 + 1 = 4 + 7	9 + 3 > 14 − 7

Read the story. Complete the picture to go with the story.

Mary planted flowers in each pot. They grew fast. She put the flowers all in a row. The white flower was in the middle. The purple flower was second. The orange flower was not first. The yellow flower was last. Where was the pink flower? Where does the orange flower go?

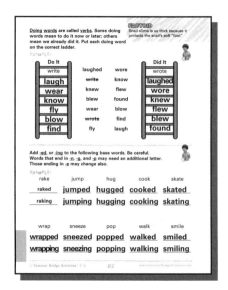

Page 82

Doing words are called verbs. Some doing words mean to do it now or later; others mean we already did it. Put each doing word on the correct ladder.

Do It / **Did It**

Add -ed, or -ing to the following base words. Be careful. Words that end in -n, -g, and -p may need an additional letter. Those ending in -e may change also.

rake	jump	hug	cook	skate
raked	jumped	hugged	cooked	skated
raking	jumping	hugging	cooking	skating

wrap	sneeze	pop	walk	smile
wrapped	sneezed	popped	walked	smiled
wrapping	sneezing	popping	walking	smiling

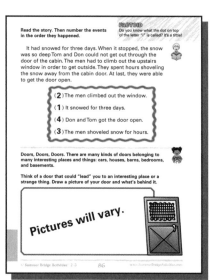

Page 83

Use a centimeter ruler. Find the length of each object.

12 cm
9 cm
8 cm
3 cm
5 cm
10 cm
4 cm

Cardinal numbers tell us how many or how much we have of something. They can be written in number (80) or word form (eighty). Ordinal numbers tell us "which one" a number is in a series. For example, if I have five apples in a row, the number three apple is the third apple in the row. (Third is an ordinal number.)

Write the number, number word, or ordinal number in the blank.

1. 70   seventy   seventieth
2. 45   forty-five   forty-fifth
3. 36   thirty-six   thirty-sixth

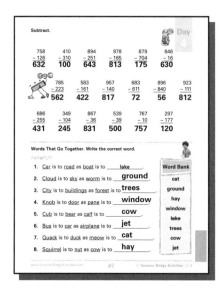

Page 84

Write these sentences correctly. Don't forget the capital letters, periods, question marks, commas, and quotation marks.

1. randy has five pets: a dog cat rabbit and two mice

Randy has five pets: a dog, cat, rabbit, and two mice.

2. do bluebirds eat seeds insects and plants

Do bluebirds eat seeds, insects, and plants?

3. would you please go to the store for me asked grayson

"Would you please go to the store for me?" asked Grayson.

4. my name is allie and i like candy

My name is Allie, and I like candy.

Write the following words under the correct heading.	(opposite) Antonyms	(sound alike) Homophones	(mean the same) Synonyms
would wood		would wood	
1. high low	high low		
2. pile heap			pile heap
3. weight wait		weight wait	
4. blend mix			blend mix
5. empty full	empty full		
6. difficult hard			difficult hard
7. rain reign		rain reign	
8. cool warm	cool warm		
9. crawl creep			crawl creep
10. groan grown		groan grown	

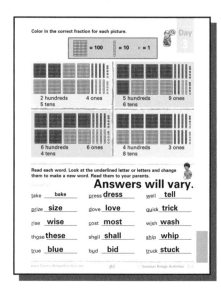

Page 85

Color in the correct fraction for each picture.

= 100   = 10   = 1

2 hundreds 5 tens   4 ones   5 hundreds 6 tens   9 ones
6 hundreds 4 tens   6 ones   6 hundreds 8 tens   3 ones

Read each word. Look at the underlined letter or letters and change them to make a new word. Read them to your parents.

Answers will vary.

take   bake   press   dress   well   tell
prize   size   dove   love   quick   trick
rise   wise   cost   most   wish   wash
those   these   shell   shall   ship   whip
true   blue   bud   bid   truck   stuck

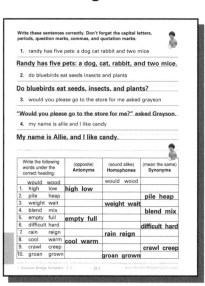

Page 86

Read the story. Then number the events in the order they happened.

It had snowed for three days. When it stopped, the snow was so deep Tom and Don could not get out through the door of the cabin. The men had to climb out the upstairs window in order to get outside. They spent hours shoveling the snow away from the cabin door. At last, they were able to get the door open.

(2) The men climbed out the window.
(1) It snowed for three days.
(4) Don and Tom got the door open.
(3) The men shoveled snow for hours.

Doors, Doors, Doors. There are many kinds of doors belonging to many interesting places and things: cars, houses, barns, bedrooms, and basements.

Think of a door that could "lead" you to an interesting place or a strange thing. Draw a picture of your door and what's behind it.

Pictures will vary.

Page 87

Subtract.

758	410	894	978	879	646
− 126	− 310	− 251	− 165	− 704	− 16
632	100	643	813	175	630

785	583	957	683	896	923
− 223	− 161	− 140	− 611	− 840	− 111
562	422	817	72	56	812

686	349	867	539	767	297
− 255	− 104	− 36	− 39	− 10	− 177
431	245	831	500	757	120

Words That Go Together. Write the correct word.

1. Car is to road as boat is to ___ lake
2. Cloud is to sky as worm is to ___ ground
3. City is to buildings as forest is to ___ trees
4. Knob is to door as pane is to ___ window
5. Cub is to bear as calf is to ___ cow
6. Bus is to car as airplane is to ___ jet
7. Quack is to duck as meow is to ___ cat
8. Squirrel is to nut as cow is to ___ hay

Word Bank
cat
ground
hay
window
lake
trees
cow
jet

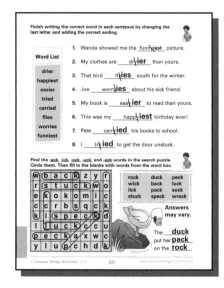

Page 88

Finish writing the correct word in each sentence by changing the last letter and adding the correct ending.

Word List
drier
happiest
easier
tried
carried
flies
worries
funniest

1. Wanda showed me the funniest picture.
2. My clothes are drier than yours.
3. That bird flies south for the winter.
4. Joe worries about his sick friend.
5. My book is easier to read than yours.
6. This was my happiest birthday ever!
7. Pete carried his books to school.
8. I tried to get the door unstuck.

Find the -ack, -ick, -ock, -uck, and -eck words in the search puzzle. Circle them. Then fill in the blanks with words from the word box.

rock   duck   peck
wick   back   luck
lick   pack   sock
stuck   speck   wreck

Answers may vary.

The duck put her pack on the rock.

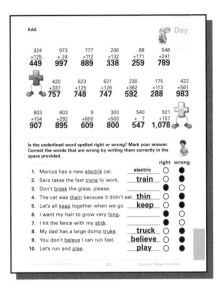

Page 89

Add.

324 +125 **449**	973 +24 **997**	777 +112 **889**	206 +132 **338**	88 +171 **259**	548 +241 **789**
420 +337 **757**	623 +125 **748**	621 +126 **747**	230 +362 **592**	175 +113 **288**	422 +561 **983**
803 +104 **907**	603 +292 **895**	9 +600 **609**	300 +500 **800**	540 +7 **547**	921 +157 **1,078**

Is the underlined word spelled right or wrong? Mark your answer. Correct the words that are wrong by writing them correctly in the space provided.

	right	wrong
1. Marcus has a new electrik car. **electric**	○	●
2. Sara takes the fast trane to work. **train**	○	●
3. Don't break the glass, please.	●	○
4. The cat was thein because it didn't eat. **thin**	○	●
5. Let's all keap together when we go. **keep**	○	●
6. I want my hair to grow very long.	●	○
7. I hit the fence with my stick.	●	○
8. My dad has a large dump truke. **truck**	○	●
9. You don't beleve I can run fast. **believe**	○	●
10. Let's run and plae. **play**	○	●

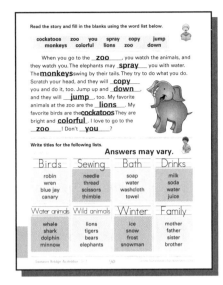

Page 90

Read the story and fill in the blanks using the word list below.

cockatoos zoo you spray copy jump
monkeys colorful lions zoo down

When you go to the **zoo**, you watch the animals, and they watch you. The elephants may **spray** you with water. The **monkeys** swing by their tails. They try to do what you do. Scratch your head, and they will **copy** you and do it, too. Jump up and **down**, and they will **jump**, too. My favorite animals at the zoo are the **lions**. My favorite birds are the **cockatoos**. They are bright and **colorful**. I love to go to the **zoo**! Don't **you**?

Write titles for the following lists.

Answers may vary.

Birds	Sewing	Bath	Drinks
robin	needle	soap	milk
wren	thread	water	soda
blue jay	scissors	washcloth	water
canary	thimble	towel	juice

Water animals	Wild animals	Winter	Family
whale	lions	ice	mother
shark	tigers	snow	father
dolphin	bears	frost	sister
minnow	elephants	snowman	brother

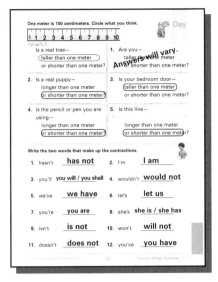

Page 91

One meter is 100 centimeters. Circle what you think.

EXAMPLE:
Is a real tree—
(taller than one meter) or shorter than one meter?

Answers will vary.

1. Are you— taller than one meter or shorter than one meter?
2. Is a real puppy— longer than one meter (or shorter than one meter)
3. Is your bedroom door— (taller than one meter) or shorter than one meter?
4. Is the pencil or pen you are using— longer than one meter (or shorter than one meter)
5. Is this line— longer than one meter (or shorter than one meter)

Write the two words that make up the contractions.

1. hasn't	**has not**	2. I'm	**I am**
3. you'll	**you will / you shall**	4. wouldn't	**would not**
5. we've	**we have**	6. let's	**let us**
7. you're	**you are**	8. she's	**she is / she has**
9. isn't	**is not**	10. won't	**will not**
11. doesn't	**does not**	12. you've	**you have**

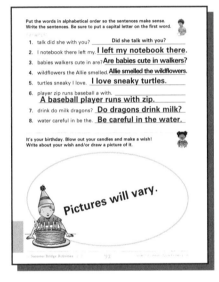

Page 92

Put the words in alphabetical order so the sentences make sense. Write the sentences. Be sure to put a capital letter on the first word.

1. talk did she with you? **Did she talk with you?**
2. I notebook there left my. **I left my notebook there.**
3. babies walkers cute in are? **Are babies cute in walkers?**
4. wildflowers the Allie smelled. **Allie smelled the wildflowers.**
5. turtles sneaky I love. **I love sneaky turtles.**
6. player zip runs baseball with a. **A baseball player runs with zip.**
7. drink do milk dragons? **Do dragons drink milk?**
8. water careful in be the. **Be careful in the water.**

It's your birthday. Blow out your candles and make a wish! Write about your wish and/or draw a picture of it.

Pictures will vary.

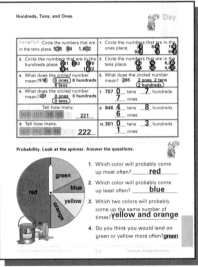

Page 93

Hundreds, Tens, and Ones.

EXAMPLE: Circle the numbers that are in the tens place. 5**3**6 **8**4 1,**6**02

1. Circle the numbers that are in the ones place. 53**6** 8**4** 1,60**2**
2. Circle the numbers that are in the hundreds place. **6**81 6**4**3 **8**70
3. Circle the numbers that are in the tens place. **2**9 6,2**1**0 4,8**4**7
4. What does the circled number mean? 51**6** 6 ones 6 hundreds 6 tens
5. What does the circled number mean? **2**65 2 ones 2 tens 2 hundreds
6. What does the circled number mean? 2**0**1 0 ones 0 hundreds 0 tens
7. 7**0**7 **7** tens **7** hundreds 7 ones
8. 84**6** 4 tens 8 hundreds **6** ones

Tell how many.
9. 100 100 10 10 **221**
10. 301 0 tens 3 hundreds 1 ones

Tell how many.
100 100 10 10 **222**

Probability. Look at the spinner. Answer the questions.

1. Which color will probably come up most often? **red**
2. Which color will probably come up least often? **blue**
3. Which two colors will probably come up the same number of times? **yellow and orange**
4. Do you think you would land on green or yellow more often? **green**

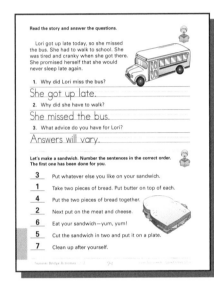

Page 94

Read the story and answer the questions.

Lori got up late today, so she missed the bus. She had to walk to school. She was tired and cranky when she got there. She promised herself that she would never sleep late again.

1. Why did Lori miss the bus?
She got up late.

2. Why did she have to walk?
She missed the bus.

3. What advice do you have for Lori?
Answers will vary.

Let's make a sandwich. Number the sentences in the correct order. The first one has been done for you.

3	Put whatever else you like on your sandwich.
1	Take two pieces of bread. Put butter on top of each.
4	Put the two pieces of bread together.
2	Next put on the meat and cheese.
6	Eat your sandwich—yum, yum!
5	Cut the sandwich in two and put it on a plate.
7	Clean up after yourself.

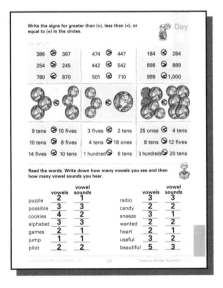

Page 95

Write the signs for greater than (>), less than (<), or equal to (=) in the circles.

EXAMPLE:

386 > 367	474 > 447	184 < 284
254 > 245	442 < 542	898 > 893
780 < 870	501 < 710	999 < 1,000

9 tens > 10 fives	3 fives < 2 tens	25 ones > 4 tens
10 tens > 8 fives	4 tens < 18 ones	8 tens > 12 fives
14 fives > 10 tens	1 hundred > 6 tens	3 hundreds > 20 tens

Read the words. Write down how many vowels you see and then how many vowel sounds you hear.

	vowels	vowel sounds		vowels	vowel sounds
puzzle	2	1	radio	3	3
possible	3	2	candy	2	2
cookies	4	2	sneeze	3	1
alphabet	3	3	wanted	2	2
games	2	1	heart	2	1
jump	1	1	useful	3	2
pilot	2	2	beautiful	5	3

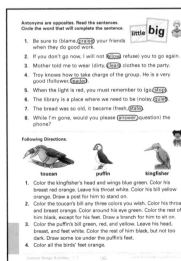

Page 96

Antonyms are opposites. Read the sentences. Circle the word that will complete the sentence.

little **big**

1. Be sure to (blame, (praise)) your friends when they do good work.
2. If you don't go now, I will not ((allow), refuse) you to go again.
3. Mother told me to wear (dirty, (clean)) clothes to the party.
4. Troy knows how to take charge of the group. He is a very good (follower, (leader)).
5. When the light is red, you must remember to (go, (stop)).
6. The library is a place where we need to be (noisy, (quiet)).
7. The bread was so old, it became (fresh, (stale)).
8. While I'm gone, would you please ((answer), question) the phone?

Following Directions.

toucan   puffin   kingfisher

1. Color the kingfisher's head and wings blue green. Color his breast red orange. Leave his bill yellow orange. Draw a post for him to stand on.
2. Color the toucan's bill any three colors you wish. Color his throat and breast orange. Color around his eye green. Color the rest of him black, except for his feet. Draw a branch for him to sit on.
3. Color the puffin's bill green, red, and yellow. Leave his head, breast, and feet white. Color the rest of him black, but not too dark. Draw some ice under the puffin's feet.
4. Color all the birds' feet orange.

Page 97

Add or subtract.

573 -132 **441**	832 +23 **855**	153 +210 **363**	637 -224 **413**	638 -532 **106**	721 +112 **833**
35 -25 **10**	263 +13 **276**	508 -305 **203**	337 +231 **568**	544 -234 **310**	206 +392 **598**
972 -421 **551**	684 -182 **502**	912 +87 **999**	400 +500 **900**	805 -202 **603**	978 -326 **652**

Find the hidden sentences and write them on the lines. Remember capital letters and periods.

1.	2.	3.
I C	D A N I	P N H I A M S O
L A	U R N M	L G M E N I A F
I N	C E Y A	A W Y N D L L F
K D	K F A L	Y I F D F Y O U
E Y	S U N S	I T R S A I T N

1. **I like candy.**
2. **Ducks are funny animals.**
3. **Playing with my friends and family is a lot of fun.**

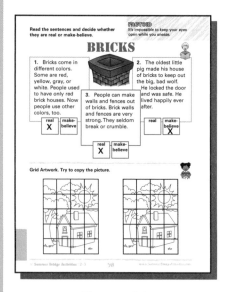

Page 98

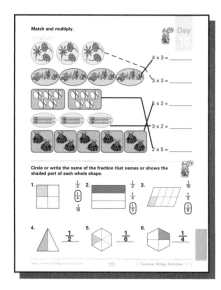

Page 99

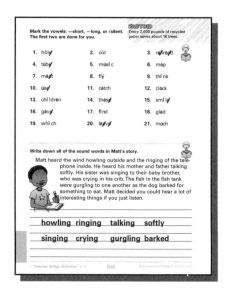

Page 100

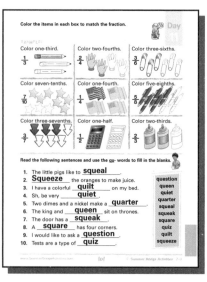

Page 101

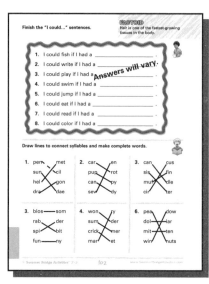

Page 102

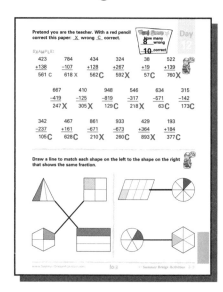

Page 103

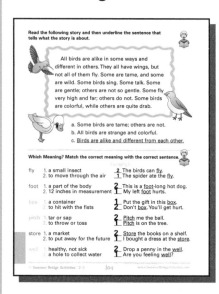

Page 104

Page 105

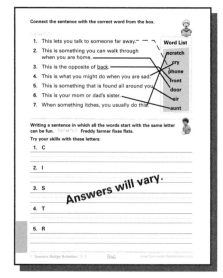

Page 106

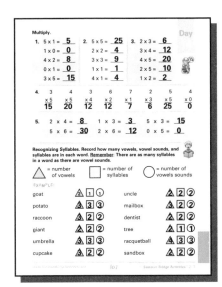

Page 107

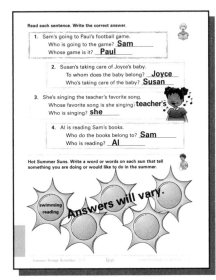

Page 108

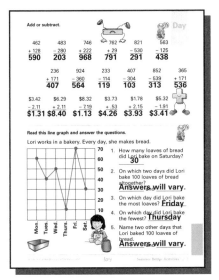

Page 109

Read the poem; then do the activity below.

My Shadow

I have a little shadow that goes in and out with me,
And what can be the use of him is more than I can see.
He is very, very like me from the heels up to the head;
And I see him jump before me, when I jump into bed.

—Robert Louis Stevenson

1. What does your shadow do when you jump into bed?

jump before me

2. Who does your shadow look like?

very, very like me

3. When do you see your shadow?

sunny, lamp light, etc.

4. What else can your shadow do besides jump?

Answers will vary.

Write yes if the sentence is complete or no if it is not.

EXAMPLE:	A. Inside a large.	No
	B. Someone is walking on the sidewalk.	Yes
1.	I went to a movie last night.	Yes
2.	We played in the park by.	No
3.	Who is going to?	No
4.	Today is my birthday.	Yes
5.	Under the swing in front of the house.	No
6.	Every Friday after school.	No
7.	Did you enjoy reading that book?	Yes
8.	Andy likes to play football.	Yes

Page 110

Better Bodies Better Behavior

Up until now, **Summer Bridge Activities**™ has been all about your mind...

But the other parts of you—who you are, how you act, and how you feel—are important too. These pages are all about helping build a better you this summer.

Keeping your body strong and healthy helps you live better, learn better, and feel better. To keep your body healthy, you need to do things like eat right, get enough sleep, and exercise. The Physical Fitness pages of Building Better Bodies will teach you about good eating habits and the importance of proper exercise. You can even train for a Presidential Fitness Award over the summer.

The Character pages are all about building a better you on the inside. They've got fun activities for you and your family to do together. The activities will help you develop important values and habits you'll need as you grow up.

After a summer of Building Better Bodies and Behavior and **Summer Bridge Activities**™, there may be a whole new you ready for school in the fall!

For Parents: Introduction to Character Education

Character education is simply giving your child clear messages about the values you and your family consider important. Many studies have shown that a basic core of values is universal. You will find certain values reflected in the laws of every country and incorporated in the teachings of religious, ethical, and other belief systems throughout the world.

The character activities included here are designed to span the entire summer. Each week your child will be introduced to a new value, with a quote and two activities that illustrate it. Research has shown that character education is most effective when parents reinforce the values in their child's daily routine; therefore, we encourage parents to be involved as their child completes the lessons.

Here are some suggestions on how to maximize these lessons.
- Read through the lesson yourself. Then set aside a block of time for you and your child to discuss the value.
- Plan a block of time to work on the suggested activities.
- Discuss the meaning of the quote with your child. Ask, "What do you think the quote means?" Have your child ask other members of the family the same question. If possible, include grandparents, aunts, uncles, and cousins.
- Use the quote as often as you can during the week. You'll be pleasantly surprised to learn that both you and your child will have it memorized by the end of the week.
- For extra motivation, you can set a reward for completing each week's activities.
- Point out to your child other people who are actively displaying a value. Example: "See how John is helping Mrs. Olsen by raking her leaves."
- Be sure to praise your child each time he or she practices a value: "Mary, it was very courteous of you to wait until I finished speaking."
- Find time in your day to talk about values. Turn off the radio in the car and chat with your children; take a walk in the evening as a family; read a story about the weekly value at bedtime; or give a back rub while you talk about what makes your child happy or sad.
- Finally, model the values you want your child to acquire. Remember, children will do as you do, not as you say.

Name _____ Date _____

How I Measure Up!

You will be filling in this page twice—once now and once at the end of the summer to see how you have grown. Have an adult help you measure yourself to fill in the blanks below.

around the neck   ____ / ____

smile   ____ / ____

neck to belly button   ____ / ____

shoulder to elbow   ____ / ____

around the wrist   ____ / ____

elbow to wrist   ____ / ____

around the waist   ____ / ____

length of longest finger   ____ / ____

waist to ankle   ____ / ____

around the knee   ____ / ____

around the ankle   ____ / ____

foot length   ____ / ____

around the neck   ____ / ____

smile   ____ / ____

neck to belly button   ____ / ____

shoulder to elbow   ____ / ____

around the wrist   ____ / ____

elbow to wrist   ____ / ____

around the waist   ____ / ____

length of longest finger   ____ / ____

waist to ankle   ____ / ____

around the knee   ____ / ____

around the ankle   ____ / ____

foot length   ____ / ____

Building Better Bodies and Behavior

128

© Summer Bridge Activities™

Nutrition

The food you eat helps your body grow. It gives you energy to work and play. Some foods give you protein or fats. Other foods provide vitamins, minerals, or carbohydrates. These are all things your body needs. Eating a variety of good foods each day will help you stay healthy. How much and what foods you need depends on many things, including whether you're a girl or boy, how active you are, and how old you are. To figure out the right amount of food for you, go to http://www.mypyramid.gov/mypyramid/index.aspx and use the Pyramid Plan Calculator. In the meantime, here are some general guidelines.

Your body needs nutrients from each food group every day.

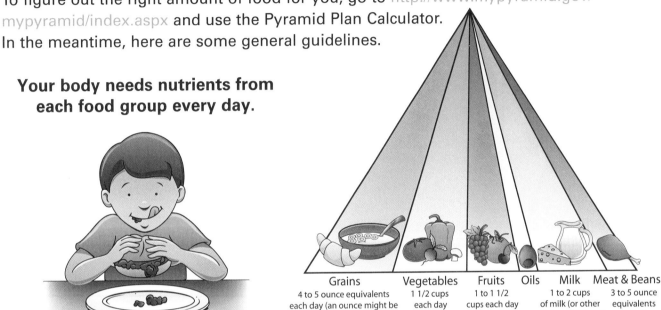

Grains
4 to 5 ounce equivalents each day (an ounce might be a slice of bread, a packet of oatmeal, or a bowl of cereal)

Vegetables
1 1/2 cups each day

Fruits
1 to 1 1/2 cups each day

Oils

Milk
1 to 2 cups of milk (or other calcium-rich food) each day

Meat & Beans
3 to 5 ounce equivalents each day

Put a ☐ around the four foods from the Grains Group.

Put a △ around the two foods from the Meat and Beans Group.

Put a ◇ around the three foods from the Milk Group.

Put a ○ around the two foods from the Fruits Group.

Put a ☐ around the four foods from the Vegetables Group.

Foods I Need Each Day

Plan out three balanced meals for one day. Arrange your meals so that by the end of the day, you will have had all the recommended amounts of food from each food group listed on the food pyramid.

Grains—4 to 5 oz. equivalents
(an ounce might be a slice of bread, a packet of oatmeal, or a bowl of cereal)

Vegetables—1 1⁄2 cups

Fruits—1 to 1 1⁄2 cups

Milk—1 to 2 cups

Meat and Beans—3 to 4 oz. equivalents
(a hamburger, half a chicken breast, or a can of tuna would be 3–4 ounces)

Draw or cut and paste pictures of the types of food you need each day.

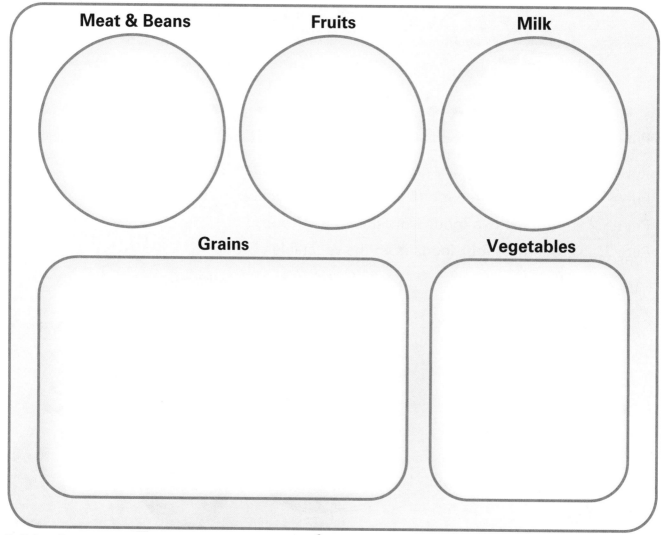

Meat & Beans **Fruits** **Milk**

Grains **Vegetables**

Meal Tracker

Use these charts to record the amount of food you eat from each food group for one or two weeks. Have another family member keep track, too, and compare.

	Grains	Milk	Meat & Beans	Fruits	Vegetables	Oils
Monday						
Tuesday						
Wednesday						
Thursday						
Friday						
Saturday						
Sunday						

	Grains	Milk	Meat & Beans	Fruits	Vegetables	Oils
Monday						
Tuesday						
Wednesday						
Thursday						
Friday						
Saturday						
Sunday						

Get Moving!

Did you know that getting no exercise can be almost as bad for you as smoking? So get moving this summer!

Summer is the perfect time to get out and get in shape. Your fitness program should include three parts:

- Get 30 minutes of aerobic exercise per day, three to five days a week.

- Exercise your muscles to improve strength and flexibility.

- Make it FUN! Do things that you like to do. Include your friends and family.

Aerobic

Strength & Flexibility

Fun

If the time you spend on activities 4 and 5 adds up to more than you spend on 1–3, you could be headed for a spud's life!

Couch Potato Quiz

1. Name three things you do each day that get you moving.

2. Name three things you do a few times a week that are good exercise.

3. How many hours do you spend each week playing outside or exercising?

4. How much TV do you watch each day?

5. How much time do you spend playing computer or video games?

You can find information on fitness at www.fitness.gov or www.kidshealth.org

Building Better Bodies and Behavior

132

© Summer Bridge Activities™

Activity Pyramid

The Activity Pyramid works like the Food Pyramid. You can use the Activity Pyramid to help plan your summer exercise program. Fill in the blanks below.

List 1 thing that isn't good exercise that you could do less of this summer.

1._____

List 3 fun activities you enjoy that get you moving and are good exercise.

1._____

2._____

3._____

List 3 exercises you could do to build strength and flexibility this summer.

1._____

2._____

3._____

Cut Down On

TV time
video or computer games
sitting for more than
30 minutes at a time

2–3 Times a Week

Work & Play
bowling
swinging
fishing
jump rope
yard work

Strength & Stretching
dancing
martial arts
gymnastics
push-ups/pull-ups

List 3 activities you would like to do for aerobic exercise this summer.

1._____

2._____

3._____

List 2 sports you would like to participate in this summer.

1._____

2._____

3–5 Times a Week
at least 30 minutes

Aerobic Exercise
walking   skating
running   bicycling
                 swimming

Sports/Recreation
soccer   relay races
basketball   tennis
volleyball   baseball

Every Day

walk
play outside
take the stairs
bathe your pet

help with chores:
sweeping
washing dishes
picking up
clothes and toys

Adapted from the President's Council on Fitness and Sports

List 5 everyday things you can do to get moving more often.

1._____

2._____

3._____

4._____

5._____

Fitness Fundamentals

Basic physical fitness includes several things:

 Cardiovascular Endurance. Your cardiovascular system includes your heart and blood vessels. You need a strong heart to pump your blood which delivers oxygen and nutrients to your body.

Muscular Strength. This is how strong your muscles are.

 **Muscular Endurance.** Endurance has to do with how long you can use your muscles before they get tired.

Flexibility. This is your ability to move your joints and to use your muscles through their full range of motion.

Body Composition. Your body is made up of lean mass and fat mass.

Lean mass includes the water, muscles, tissues, and organs in your body.

Fat mass includes the fat your body stores for energy. Exercise helps you burn body fat and maintain good body composition.

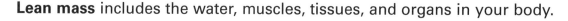

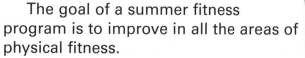

The goal of a summer fitness program is to improve in all the areas of physical fitness.

You build cardiovascular endurance through **aerobic** exercise. For **aerobic** exercise, you need to work large muscle groups at a steady pace. This increases your heart rate and breathing. You can jog, walk, hike, swim, dance, do aerobics, ride a bike, go rowing, climb stairs, rollerblade, play golf, backpack...

You should get at least 30 minutes of aerobic exercise per day, three to five days a week.

You build muscular strength and endurance with exercises that work your muscles, like sit-ups, push-ups, pull-ups, and weight lifting.

You can increase flexibility through stretching exercises. These are good for warm-ups, too.

Draw a stick person. Give your person a heart (for aerobic exercise), muscles in the arms (for strength and endurance), and bent knees (for flexibility).

Your Summer Fitness Program

Start your summer fitness program by choosing at least one aerobic activity from your Activity Pyramid. You can choose more than one for variety.

Do this activity three to five times each week. Keep it up for at least 30 minutes each time.
(Exercise hard enough to increase your heart rate and your breathing. Don't exercise so hard that you get dizzy or can't catch your breath.)

Use this chart to plan when you will exercise, or use it as a record when you exercise.

DATE	ACTIVITY	TIME

DATE	ACTIVITY	TIME

Plan a reward for meeting your exercise goals for two weeks.
(You can make copies of this chart to track your fitness all summer long.)

Start Slow!

Remember to start out slow. Exercise is about getting stronger. It's not about being superman—or superwoman—right off the bat.

Are You Up to the Challenge?

The Presidential Physical Fitness Award Program was designed to help kids get into shape and have fun. To earn the award, you take five fitness tests. These are usually given by teachers at school, but you can train for them this summer. Make a chart to track your progress. Keep working all summer to see if you can improve your score.

Remember: Start Slow!

1. Curl-ups. Lie on the floor with your knees bent and your feet about 12 inches from your buttocks. Cross your arms over your chest. Raise your trunk up and touch your elbows to your thighs. Do as many as you can in one minute.

2. Shuttle Run. Draw a starting line. Put two blocks 30 feet away. Run the 30 feet, pick up a block, and bring it back to the starting line. Then run and bring back the second block. Record your fastest time.

3. V-sit Reach. Sit on the floor with your legs straight and your feet 8 to 12 inches apart. Put a ruler between your feet, pointing past your toes. Have a partner hold your legs straight, and keep your toes pointed up. Link your thumbs together and reach forward, palms down, as far as you can along the ruler.

4. One-Mile Walk/Run. On a track or some safe area, run one mile. You can walk as often as you need to. Finish as fast as possible. (Ages six to seven may want to run a quarter mile; ages eight to nine, half a mile.)

5. Pull-ups. Grip a bar with an overhand grip (the backs of your hands toward your face). Have someone lift you up if you need help. Hang with your arms and legs straight. Pull your body up until your chin is over the bar; then let yourself back down. Do as many as you can.

Respect

Respect is showing good manners toward all people, not just those you know or who are like you. Respect is treating everyone, no matter what religion, race, or culture, male or female, rich or poor, in a way that you would want to be treated. The easiest way to do this is to decide to **never** take part in activities and to **never** use words that make fun of people because they are different from you or your friends.

Treat others as you would like to be treated.

~ The Golden Rule

Color the picture below.

Activity

This week go to the library and check out *Bein' with You This Way* by W. Nikola-Lisa (1995). This book is a fun rap about things that make us different and things that make us the same. Read it with your parents!

Gratitude

Gratitude is when you thank people for the good things they have given you or done for you. Thinking about people and events in your life that make you feel grateful (thankful) will help you become a happier person.

There are over 465 different ways of saying thank you. Here are a few:

Danke *Toda* *Merci* Gracias **Nandri**

Spasibo Arigato **Gadda ge** Paldies Hvala

Make a list of ten things you are grateful for.

1. _____
2. _____
3. _____
4. _____
5. _____

6. _____
7. _____
8. _____
9. _____
10. _____

A Recipe for Saying Thanks

1. Make a colorful card.
2. On the inside, write a thank-you note to someone who has done something nice for you.
3. Address an envelope to that person.
4. Pick out a cool stamp.
5. Drop your note in the nearest mailbox.

Saying thank you creates love.

~ Daphne Rose Kingma

Manners

If you were the only person in the world, you wouldn't have to have **good manners** or be **courteous**. However, there are over six billion people on our planet, and good manners help us all get along with each other.

Children with good manners are usually well liked by other children and are certainly liked by adults. Here are some simple rules for good manners:

- When you ask for something, say, "Please."
- When someone gives you something, say, "Thank you."
- When someone says, "Thank you," say, "You're welcome."
- If you walk in front of someone or bump into a person, say, "Excuse me."
- When someone else is talking, wait before speaking.
- Share and take turns.

No kindness, no matter how small, is ever wasted. ~ Aesop's Fables

See How I'm Nice

(sung to "Three Blind Mice")

See how I'm nice,
see how I'm nice.
Thanks, thanks, thanks.
Please, please, please.
I cover my nose whenever I sneeze.
I sit on my chair, not on my knees.
I always say "thank you" when
I'm passed some peas.
Thanks, thanks, thanks.
Please, please, please.

I've Got Manners

Make a colorful poster to display on your bedroom door or on the refrigerator. List five ways you are going to practice your manners. Be creative and decorate with watercolors, poster paints, pictures cut from magazines, clip art, or geometric shapes.

Instead of making a poster, you could make a mobile to hang from your ceiling that shows five different manners to practice.

Choices

A **choice** is when you get to pick between two or more things. Often, one choice is better for you than another. Spend time thinking about which choice would be best for you before you make a decision.

Let's Practice. Pick which you think is the best choice:

1. What might be best for you to eat?
   a. an apple   b. a candy bar   c. potato chips

2. What is a good time to go to bed on a school night?
   a. midnight   b. 8:00 P.M.   c. noon

3. If a friend pushes you, you should
   a. cry.   b. hit him/her.   c. tell your friend, in a nice voice, that you don't like being pushed.

Activity

Get a copy of *The Tale of Peter Rabbit* by Beatrix Potter. Read it out loud with an adult. Talk about the choices Peter made during the story. Are there other choices that would have been better?

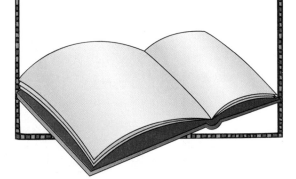

Color the picture below.

Friendship

Friends come in all sizes, shapes, and ages: brothers, sisters, parents, neighbors, good teachers, and school and sports friends.

There is a saying, "To have a friend you need to be a friend." Can you think of a day when someone might have tried to get you to say or do unkind things to someone else? Sometimes it takes courage to be a real friend. Did you have the courage to say no?

A Recipe for Friendship

1 cup of always listening to ideas and stories
2 pounds of never talking behind a friend's back
1 pound of no mean teasing
2 cups of always helping a friend who needs help

Take these ingredients and mix completely together. Add laughter, kindness, hugs, and even tears. Bake for as long as it takes to make your friendship good and strong.

It's so much more friendly with two.

~ A. A. Milne
(creator of Winnie the Pooh)

Family Night at the Movies

Rent *Toy Story* or *Toy Story II*. Each movie is a simple, yet powerful, tale about true friendship. Fix a big bowl of popcorn to share with your family during the show.

International Friendship Day

The first Sunday in August is International Friendship Day. This is a perfect day to remember all your friends and how they have helped you during your friendship. Give your friends a call or send them an email or snail-mail card.

Confidence

People are **confident** or have **confidence** when they feel like they can succeed at a certain task. To feel confident about doing something, most people need to practice a task over and over.

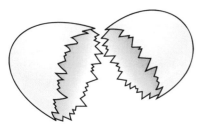

Reading, pitching a baseball, writing in cursive, playing the flute, even mopping a floor are all examples of tasks that need to be practiced before people feel confident they can succeed.

What are five things you feel confident doing?

What is one thing you want to feel more confident doing?

Make a plan for how and when you will practice until you feel confident.

You Crack Me Up!

Materials needed:
1 dozen eggs
a mixing bowl

Cracking eggs without breaking the yolk or getting egg whites all over your hands takes practice.

1. Watch an adult break an egg into the bowl. How did they hold their hands? How did they pull the egg apart?

2. Now you try. Did you do a perfect job the first time? Keep trying until you begin to feel confident about cracking eggs.

3. Use the eggs immediately to make a cheese omelet or custard pie. Refrigerate any unused eggs for up to three days.

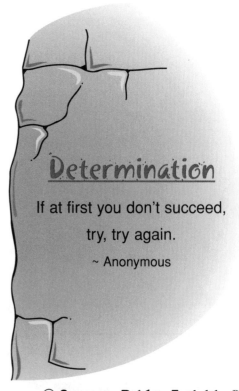

Determination

If at first you don't succeed,

try, try again.

~ Anonymous

Responsibility

You show **responsibility** by doing what you agree or promise to do. It might be a task, such as a homework assignment, or a chore, such as feeding your fish.

When you are young, your parents and teachers will give you simple tasks like putting away toys or brushing your teeth without being asked. As you get older, you will be given more responsibility. You might be trusted to come home from a friend's house at a certain time or drive to the store for groceries.

It takes a lot of practice to grow up to be a responsible person. The easiest way to practice is by keeping your promises and doing what you know is right.

A parent is responsible for different things than a child or a teenager. Write three activities you are responsible for every day. Then write three things a parent is responsible for every day.

If you want your eggs hatched, sit on them yourself. ~ Haitian Proverb

Activity

Materials needed:
21 pennies or counters such as beans, rocks, or marbles
2 small containers labeled #1 and #2

Decide on a reward for successfully completing this activity.

Put all the counters in container #1.

Review the three activities you are responsible for every day.

Each night before you go to bed, put one counter for each completed activity into container #2. At the end of seven days count all the counters in container #2.

If you have 16 or more counters in container #2, you are on your way to becoming very responsible. Collect your reward.

My reward is_____.

Service/Helping

Service is **helping** another person or group of people without asking for any kind of reward or payment. These are some good things that happen when you do service:

1. You feel closer to the people in your community (neighborhood).
2. You feel pride in yourself when you see that you can help other people in need.
3. Your family feels proud of you.
4. You will make new friends as you help others.

An old saying goes, "Charity begins at home." This means that you don't have to do big, important-sounding things to help people. You can start in your own home and neighborhood.

Activity

Each day this week, do one act of service around your house. Don't ask for or take any kind of payment or reward. Be creative! Possible acts of service are

1. Carry in the groceries, do the dishes, or fold the laundry.
2. Read aloud to a younger brother or sister.
3. Make breakfast or pack lunches.
4. Recycle newspapers and cans.
5. Clean the refrigerator or your room.

At the end of the week, think of a project to do with your family that will help your community. You could play musical instruments or sing at a nursing home, set up a lemonade stand and give the money you make to the Special Olympics, offer to play board games with children in the hospital, or pick some flowers and take them to a neighbor. The list goes on and on.

Color the picture below.

> **Actions speak louder than words.**
> ~ Anonymous

Honesty and Trust

Being an **honest** person means you don't steal, cheat, or tell lies. **Trust** is when you believe someone will be honest. If you are dishonest, or not truthful, people will not trust you.

You want to tell the truth because it is important to have your family and friends trust you. However, it takes courage to tell the truth, especially if you don't want people to get mad at you or be disappointed in the way you behaved.

How would your parents feel if you lied to them? People almost always find out about lies, and most parents will be more angry about a lie than if you had told them the truth in the first place.

When family or friends ask about something, remember that honesty is telling the truth. Honesty is telling what really happened. Honesty is keeping your promises. *Be proud of being an honest person.*

Color the picture.

Parent note: Help your child by pointing out times he or she acted honestly.

Count to Ten

Tape ten pieces of colored paper to your refrigerator. For one week, each time you tell the truth or keep a promise, take one piece of paper down and put it in the recycling bin. If all ten pieces of paper are gone by the end of the week, collect your reward.

> **Honesty is the first chapter in the book of wisdom.**
> ~ Thomas Jefferson

Most Improved

My reward is _____.

Happiness

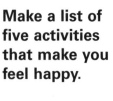

Happiness is a feeling that comes when you enjoy your life. Different things make different people happy. Some people feel happy when they are playing soccer. Other people feel happy when they are playing the cello. It is important to understand what makes you happy so you can include some of these things in your daily plan.

These are some actions that show you are happy: laughing, giggling, skipping, smiling, and hugging.

Make a list of five activities that make you feel happy.

1
2
3
4
5

Bonus!

List two things you could do to make someone else happy.

1._____

2._____

Activity

Write down a plan to do one activity each day this week that makes you happy.

Try simple things—listen to your favorite song, play with a friend, bake muffins, shoot hoops, etc.

Be sure to thank everyone who helps you, and don't forget to laugh!

Happy Thought

The world is so full

of a number of things,

I'm sure we should

all be happy as kings.

~Robert Louis Stevenson

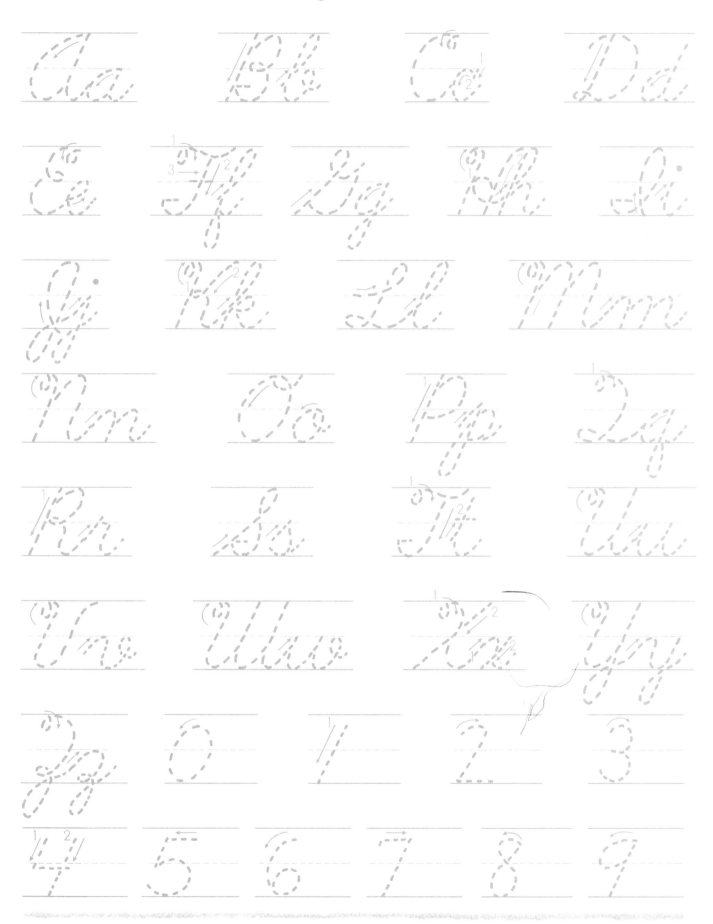

 **Practice writing below.**

Aa *Bb* *Cc* *Dd*

Ee *Ff* *Gg* *Hh* *Ii*

Jj *Kk* *Ll* *Mm*

Nn *Oo* *Pp* *Qq*

Rr *Ss* *Tt* *Uu*

Vv *Ww* *Xx* *Yy*

Zz *0* *1* *2* *3*

4 *5* *6* *7* *8* *9*

Addition and Subtraction (0-18)

Developing math skills can be a challenging experience for both parent and child.

- **Have a positive attitude.**
- **Relax and enjoy the learning process.**
- **Keep the learning time short and fun you will get better results.**
- **Review the cards with your child.**
- **Read the front of the card.**
- **Check your answer on the reverse side.**
- **Separate those he/she does not know.**
- **Review those he/she does know.**
- **Gradually work through the other cards.**

These steps will help build your child's confidence with addition and subtraction. Enjoy the rewards!

"Teacher, Teacher"

Three or more players.
Each player takes a turn as "Teacher."
The Teacher mixes up the flashcards and holds one card up at a time.
First player to yell out "Teacher, Teacher,"
will have the first chance to give the answer.
If his/her answer is right he/she receives 5 points.
If his/her answer is wrong, he/she will not receive any points.
Move on to the next person until someone answers correctly.
The next round someone else is teacher.
Repeat each round.
Reward the different levels; everyone wins!

Time Challenge

Follow the directions for "Teacher, Teacher" and add a time to it.
Increase the point system to meet the Time Challenge.
Reward the different levels, everyone wins!

0 + 0	2 + 0	4 + 0	5 + 0
3	2	1	0
8 + 0	0 + 1	1 + 1	2 + 1
7	6	5	4
5 + 1	7 + 1	9 + 1	2 + 2
1	0	9	8

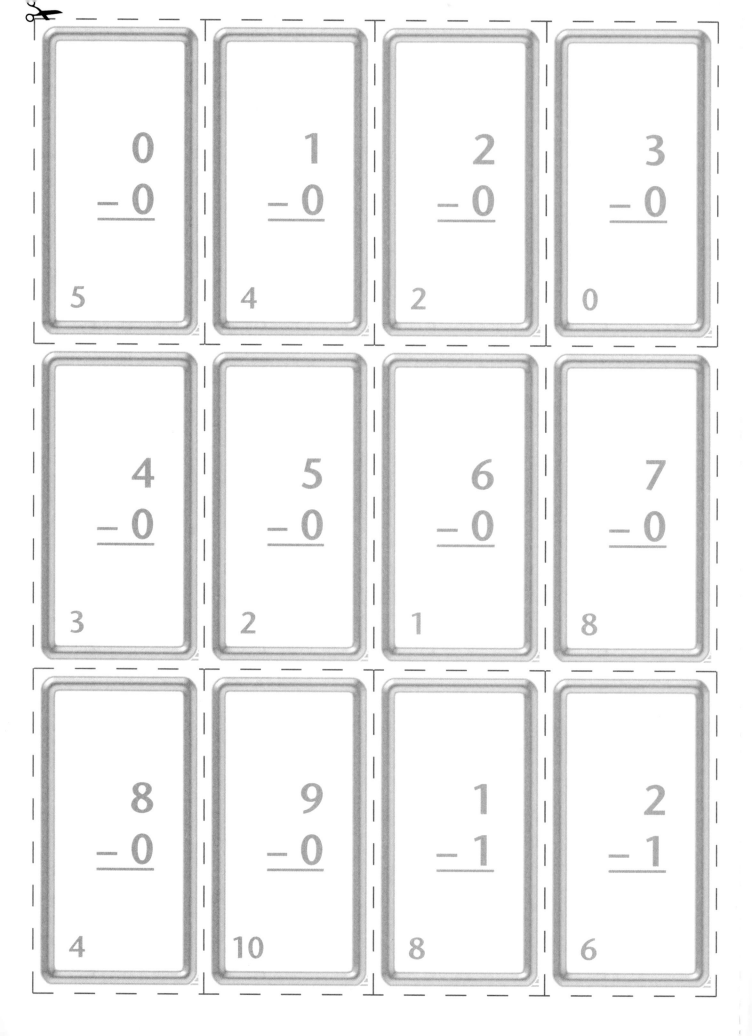

0 − 0 ─ 5	1 − 0 ─ 4	2 − 0 ─ 2	3 − 0 ─ 0
4 − 0 ─ 3	5 − 0 ─ 2	6 − 0 ─ 1	7 − 0 ─ 8
8 − 0 ─ 4	9 − 0 ─ 10	1 − 1 ─ 8	2 − 1 ─ 6

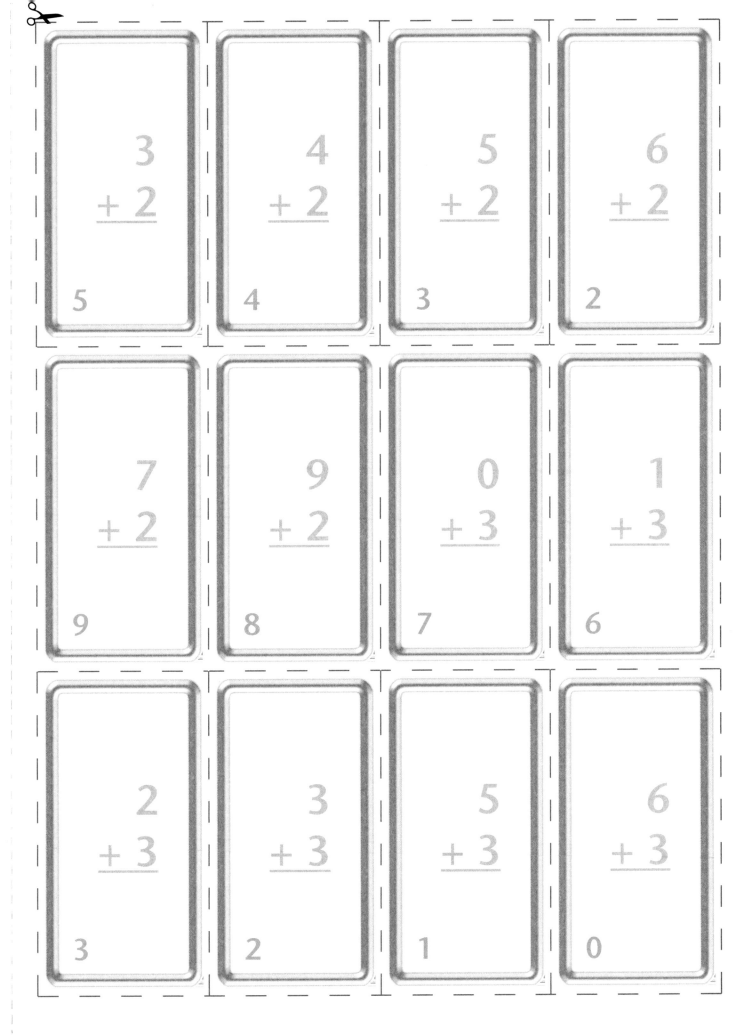

3 + 2 5	4 + 2 4	5 + 2 3	6 + 2 2
7 + 2 9	9 + 2 8	0 + 3 7	1 + 3 6
2 + 3 3	3 + 3 2	5 + 3 1	6 + 3 0

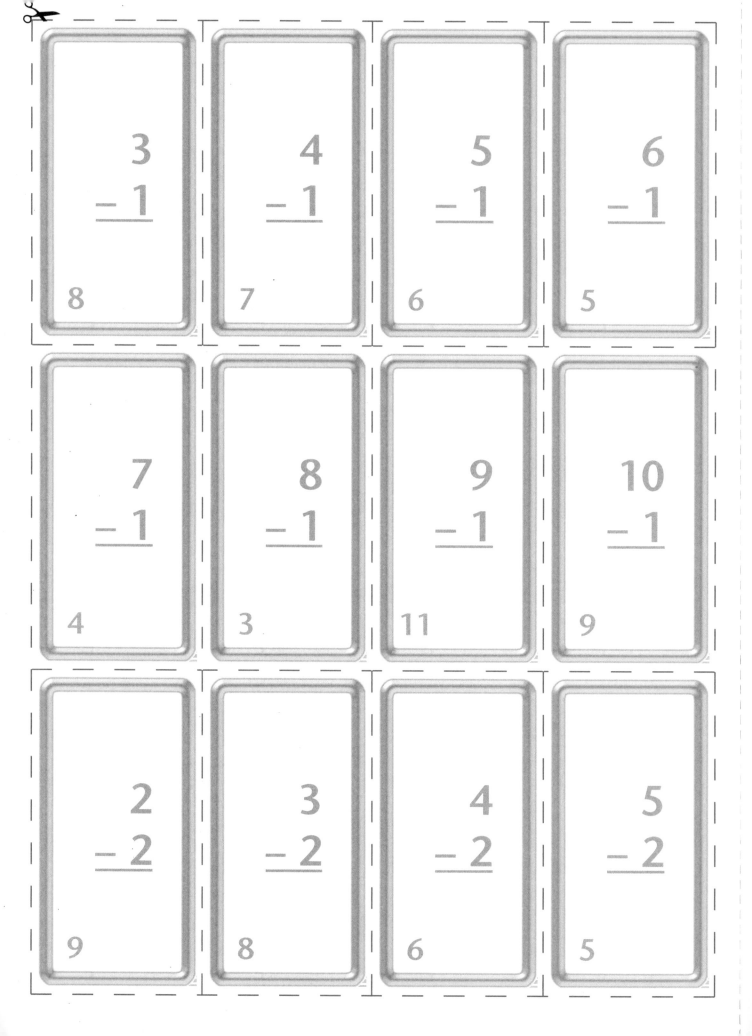

3	4	5	6
− 1	− 1	− 1	− 1
8	7	6	5

7	8	9	10
− 1	− 1	− 1	− 1
4	3	11	9

2	3	4	5
− 2	− 2	− 2	− 2
9	8	6	5

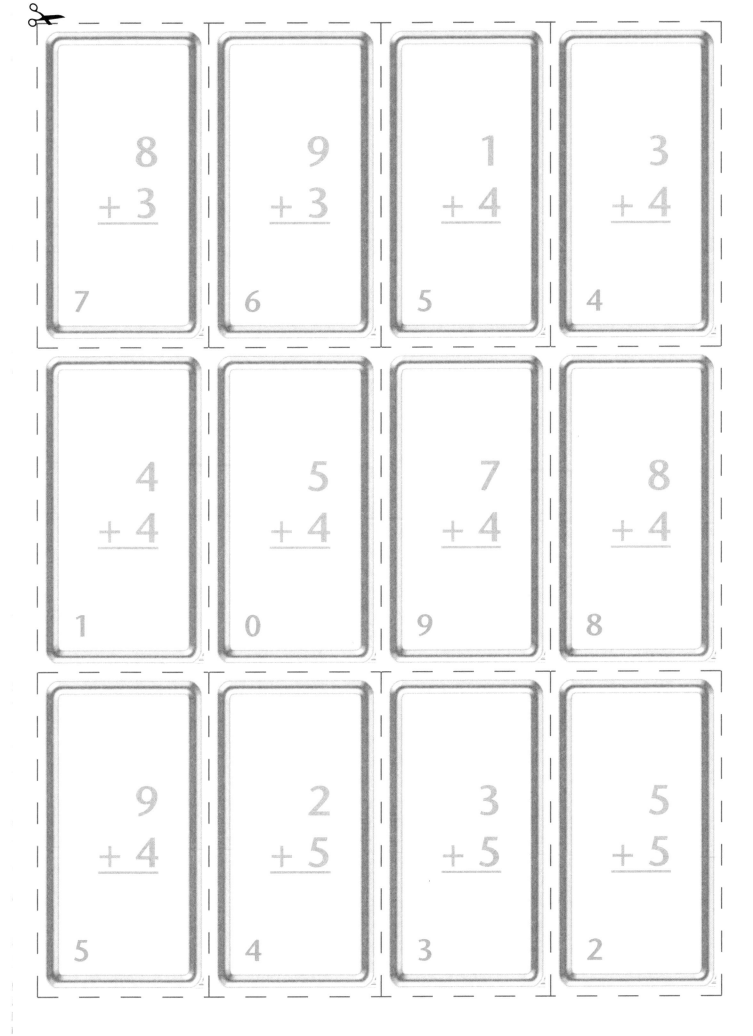

8
+ 3

7

9
+ 3

6

1
+ 4

5

3
+ 4

4

4
+ 4

1

5
+ 4

0

7
+ 4

9

8
+ 4

8

9
+ 4

5

2
+ 5

4

3
+ 5

3

5
+ 5

2

$\begin{array}{r} 6 \\ -\ 2 \\ \hline \end{array}$ 7	$\begin{array}{r} 7 \\ -\ 2 \\ \hline \end{array}$ 5	$\begin{array}{r} 8 \\ -\ 2 \\ \hline \end{array}$ 12	$\begin{array}{r} 9 \\ -\ 2 \\ \hline \end{array}$ 11
$\begin{array}{r} 10 \\ -\ 2 \\ \hline \end{array}$ 12	$\begin{array}{r} 11 \\ -\ 2 \\ \hline \end{array}$ 11	$\begin{array}{r} 3 \\ -\ 3 \\ \hline \end{array}$ 9	$\begin{array}{r} 4 \\ -\ 3 \\ \hline \end{array}$ 8
$\begin{array}{r} 5 \\ -\ 3 \\ \hline \end{array}$ 10	$\begin{array}{r} 6 \\ -\ 3 \\ \hline \end{array}$ 8	$\begin{array}{r} 7 \\ -\ 3 \\ \hline \end{array}$ 7	$\begin{array}{r} 8 \\ -\ 3 \\ \hline \end{array}$ 13

7 + 5	8 + 5	9 + 5	1 + 6
9	8	7	6
2 + 6	4 + 6	5 + 6	6 + 6
3	2	1	0
7 + 6	8 + 6	0 + 7	1 + 7
7	6	5	4

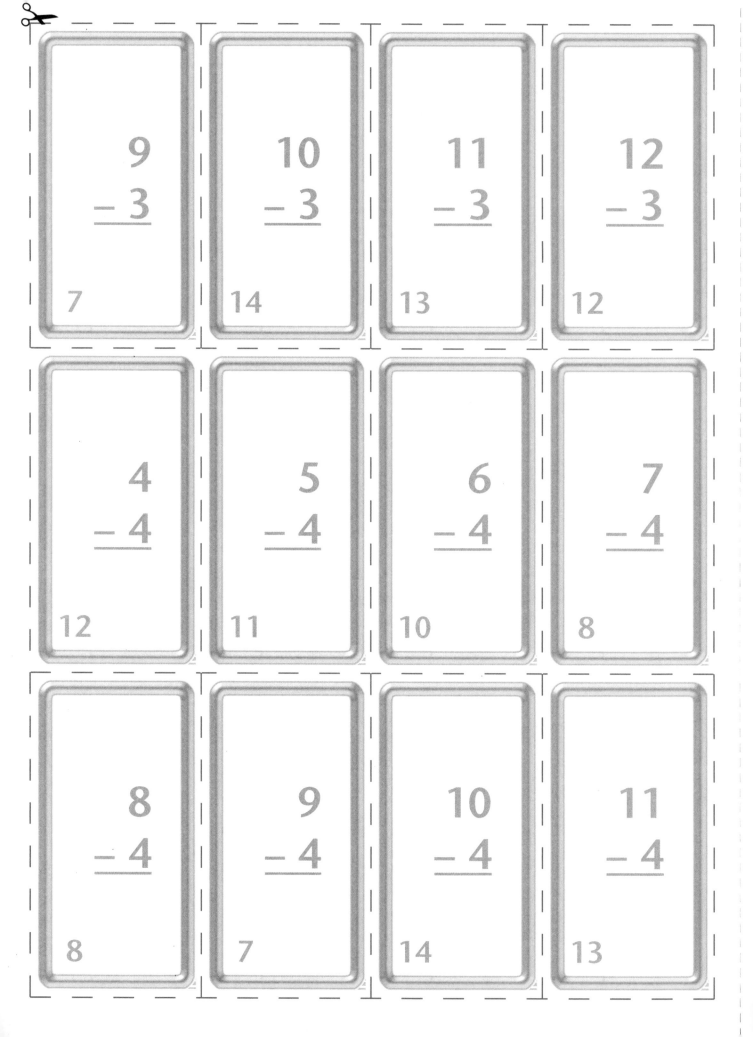

$\begin{array}{r} 9 \\ -\ 3 \\ \hline \end{array}$	$\begin{array}{r} 10 \\ -\ 3 \\ \hline \end{array}$	$\begin{array}{r} 11 \\ -\ 3 \\ \hline \end{array}$	$\begin{array}{r} 12 \\ -\ 3 \\ \hline \end{array}$
7	14	13	12
$\begin{array}{r} 4 \\ -\ 4 \\ \hline \end{array}$	$\begin{array}{r} 5 \\ -\ 4 \\ \hline \end{array}$	$\begin{array}{r} 6 \\ -\ 4 \\ \hline \end{array}$	$\begin{array}{r} 7 \\ -\ 4 \\ \hline \end{array}$
12	11	10	8
$\begin{array}{r} 8 \\ -\ 4 \\ \hline \end{array}$	$\begin{array}{r} 9 \\ -\ 4 \\ \hline \end{array}$	$\begin{array}{r} 10 \\ -\ 4 \\ \hline \end{array}$	$\begin{array}{r} 11 \\ -\ 4 \\ \hline \end{array}$
8	7	14	13

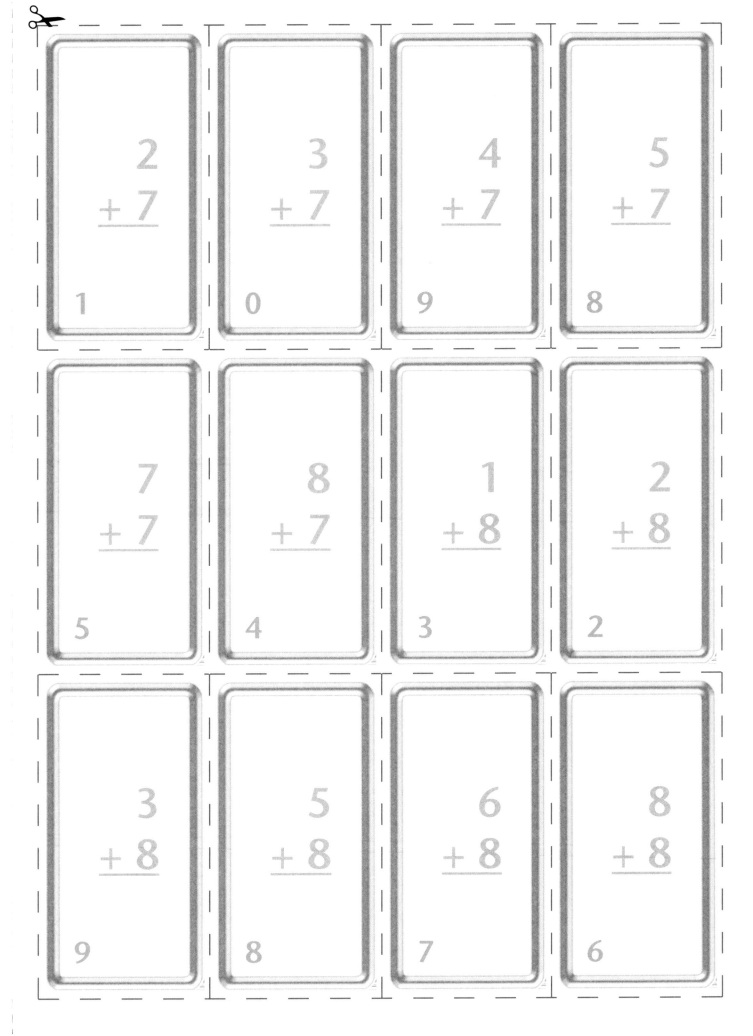

2
+ 7

1

3
+ 7

0

4
+ 7

9

5
+ 7

8

7
+ 7

5

8
+ 7

4

1
+ 8

3

2
+ 8

2

3
+ 8

9

5
+ 8

8

6
+ 8

7

8
+ 8

6

12	13	5	6
− 4	− 4	− 5	− 5
12	11	10	9

7	8	9	10
− 5	− 5	− 5	− 5
10	9	15	14

11	12	13	14
− 5	− 5	− 5	− 5
16	14	13	11

9 + 8	0 + 9	2 + 9	4 + 9
7	6	5	4
6 + 9	7 + 9	8 + 9	9 + 9
1	0	9	8
6 − 6	7 − 6	8 − 6	9 − 6
5	4	3	2

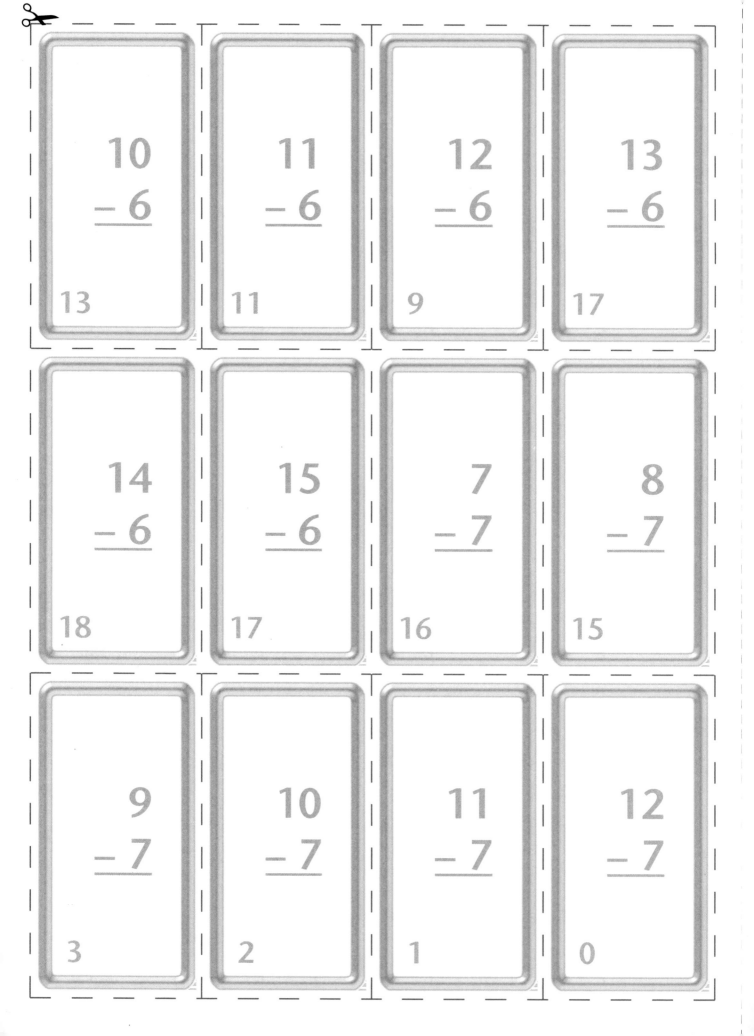

10 − 6	11 − 6	12 − 6	13 − 6
13	11	9	17
14 − 6	15 − 6	7 − 7	8 − 7
18	17	16	15
9 − 7	10 − 7	11 − 7	12 − 7
3	2	1	0

13 − 7	14 − 7	15 − 7	16 − 7
1	0	9	8
8 − 8	9 − 8	10 − 8	11 − 8
5	4	3	2
12 − 8	13 − 8	14 − 8	15 − 8
9	8	7	6

16
− 8

9

17
− 8

8

9
− 9

7

10
− 9

6

11
− 9

3

12
− 9

2

13
− 9

1

14
− 9

0

15
− 9

7

16
− 9

6

17
− 9

5

18
− 9

4

Congratulations!

_____
your name

HAS COMPLETED

Summer Bridge Activities™

AND IS READY FOR THE 3RD GRADE!

Ms. Hansen

Ms. Hansen

Mr. Fredrickson

Mr. Fredrickson

Parent's Signature

WWW.SUMMER BRIDGE ACTIVITIES.COM